Information Insecurity

A survival guide to the uncharted territories of cyber-threats and cyber-security

Eduardo Gelbstein
Ahmad Kamal

United Nations

United Nations Information and Communication Technologies Task Force

Published by the
United Nations ICT Task Force
and the
United Nations Institute for Training and Research
One United Nations Plaza
New York, NY 10017

First Edition: September 2002
Second Edition: November 2002

The opinions expressed in this book are those of the authors and do not necessarily reflect the views of the United Nations or of any other United Nations organs and agencies referred to in this book.

© All rights reserved
No part of the material in this book and its accompanying CD-ROM may be reproduced in any form without the written permission of the authors.

PREFACE

This book is presented to the Member States of the United Nations by the United Nations ICT Task Force and the United Nations Institute of Training and Research (UNITAR) as part of their respective ongoing programmes in the field of Information Technology, including the Policy Awareness and Training in Information Technology seminars organised jointly for Ambassadors and Diplomats in New York.

The subject of the book, namely, Information Insecurity, is most timely, as attention focuses more than ever before towards the dangers inherent in the new opportunities for good and evil that have been opened up in Information Technology.

This is a thought provoking book. The two co-authors are to be congratulated in setting the problem out clearly for all to see and work upon. Hopefully, the book will encourage further movement in the near future along the suggested lines.

Jose-Maria Figueres *Marcel Boisard*
Jose Maria Figueres Marcel Boisard
Chairman Executive Director
United Nations United Nations
ICT Task Force Institute of Training and Research

TABLE OF CONTENTS

Introduction   1

The Problem   5
The nature of the beast   5
Setting the scene   6
Information security principles   13
Information security players   19
Hiding in cyber-space   35
Information security offences   39
A short history of hacking   47

The Solution   60
Managing information security   60
ISO code of practice for information security   64
Information security in the corporate environment   70
Guidelines for safe computing   80
Responding to a security incident   94
Observations and experiences   105

The Action Plan   108
Standards and Best Practices   108
Current national and regional legislation   114
Global international legislation   119
The Law of Cyber-Space   122

Recommendations   125

References   127

Appendices
Useful websites   129
Glossary   142

CD-ROM (electronic version and related presentations)

INTRODUCTION

There are many reasons why this book should be read by all, but the current and impending natures of cyber-threats are the most important ones.

Despite the understandable current emphasis on cyber-terrorism, the impact of these cyber-threats and cyber-attacks goes far deeper into the economic and social fabric of life around the world, and can affect not just peace and security, but also the success of failure of all our developmental efforts. Enormous damage can be caused not just by an act, but also by the panic, the loss of confidence, the injection of doubts and hesitations, and the destruction of trust, all of which are the primary factors on which modern society is constructed.

A major aspect of this new threat arises from the nature and pervasive spread of criminal motivation. As we know all too well, it is virtually impossible to monitor motivations. The latter are universal and invisible, and largely undetectable.

A problem lies of course in the fact that motivated individuals are highly creative. That creativity remains visible even in their warped motivations. That is why the motivation of the thief is always greater than the motivation of the detective. The criminal is always a couple of jumps ahead of the policeman. As and when the law plugs any of its numerous loopholes, the motivated criminal will always discover new cracks in the armor.

The most important defense in cyber-space is thus twofold. First, to begin with a correct analysis of one's own vulnerabilities. Second, to try to determine the opponent's motivations.

Vulnerability and motivation are then the two keys to a correct understanding of and reaction to the dangers of cyber-threats and cyber-attack.

The wide and pervasive integration of computers and embedded chips into modern society is what makes it vulnerable to cyber-attacks. Computers are now integrated into the management and processing of our daily actions, and embedded chips are so omnipresent today that it is virtually impossible to determine even their actual numbers and locations.

This profound integration of computers and information technology is obviously the strength of modern life, but it is also its vulnerability. The greater the vulnerability, the greater the ease with which it can be exploited.

The motivation to commit cyber-crime is also increasing exponentially. The number of malicious code attacks reported by the CERT has gone up from just 8 in 1988 to almost 53,000 in 2001, and the graph shows a constantly steepening increase. The first half of the year 2002 shows a 26 percent increase over the same period of the previous year.

Add to that the simple fact of its tempting results. Where the average bank hold-up brings in no more than $ 14,000, the average computer technology theft is of the order of magnitude of no less than $ 2 million. The temptation is just too great.

The status of how much is lost annually as the result of cyber-crime is unclear. Only a minute portion of computer crime gets reported. Most corporations have a well-defined tendency to conceal the manner and depth of the attacks on their facilities, for fear of the panic effect that this information would create on their stock prices.

In short, reported incidents are just the tip of the iceberg. On the one hand, the true cyber-criminal has no interest in advertising his successes, while on the other hand, the victims are afraid of reporting them also. So the environment is entirely propitious for further damage.

A distinguishing feature of cyber-crime lies in the fact that the single unattached criminal – the hacker, or the virus spreader – is really not the main danger. That is of course what hits the tabloids, partly because of the Robin Hood syndrome, and partly because it is considered "fun" among the software-literate youth. The actual minefield lies, however, in "organized" cyber-crime and cyber-terrorism, where the technical competence of youth is exploited and channeled by organised elements towards criminal and politically motivated ends.

Whereas the single hacker can work alone, organised crime requires proper networking through lines of communication between component elements. The need for those lines of communication is its vulnerability, so that is where the counter-terrorism efforts will have to concentrate.

This book is an attempt to highlight the techniques that cyber-criminals are likely to use as their primary means of communication in the current state of the technology. Most of them are known, like untraceable emails, encryption, digital compression, steganography, etc., but others will turn up as the technology evolves, as it inevitably will. All these holes will have to be plugged.

The response of the law-abiding society will not be easy. The cyber world is ethereal in its nature, and largely uncontrollable in its anarchy. The Internet was after all designed initially as a non-linear means of communication that would survive any nuclear attack. That is what makes it indestructible. By the same token, it also becomes uncontrollable, a characteristic which makes it an asset for criminal behavior.

Although many nations have written legislation against crimes committed over the Internet, such as hacking, illegal transfers of funds, identity theft, etc., the laws just cannot keep up with the technological advancements. The lure of the criminal mind and the opportunities are just too great. Add the fact that in many recent cases, the sentences have been minimal. This is virgin territory for the individual criminal, and even more attractive territory for the organized criminal.

Every technical advance in human history has been mirrored in the techniques used by criminals. The expansion of human effort into the cyber-sphere will be no different. In fact it has already started. Cyber-crime and cyber-terrorism, and possibly cyber-war, will be an inevitable part of our future landscape.

We will of course continue to enjoy the benefits of the Information Age, but we must also remain constantly aware of the dangers and pervasive pitfalls of cyber-theft, cyber-threats, cyber-crime, and of course of cyber-terrorism and cyber-war. Any or all of these can hit each one of us at any time. So, read and be warned, and prepare for the inevitable negotiations that must soon start on developing, drafting, and adopting, a comprehensive Law of Cyber-Space.

THE PROBLEM

Our first task obviously is to identify how vulnerable we are, not just in general terms, but also in its full detail.

This is difficult enough for the individual. It is even more complex for the decision maker, who has to decide on the level of acceptable residual risk and ensure that the whole organisation works to achieve it.

Many of these decision makers belong to an older age group, and are only reluctantly adjusting themselves to the revolution in information technology. Most also believe that IT is only a tool; few understand it as the beast that it really is.

1. THE NATURE OF THE BEAST

Humanity has defined itself as different from the rest of the animal kingdom. Scientists state that human DNA differs by less than 2 percent from that of the chimpanzee, the primate whose DNA resembles most closely that of a human. This small percentage accounts for some very important differences:
- Complex speech, language
- The ability to create tools
- Music, poetry, graphical arts and writing

Another difference, perhaps the most important from the perspective of security is in the use of tools: they can also be used as weapons.

Even before the invention of writing, the oral tradition passed stories from one generation to the next. Some became part of literature, such as the Iliad, describing the Trojan War; some became part of religious texts, such as the Book of Genesis, which includes the killing of Abel by his brother Cain.

Reading the history of humanity reveals that the "ascent of man" through the exploration of the world and the skies through science and technology has many believe that this knowledge and tools are for the benefit of mankind as a whole.

Many others see science and technology as the source of improved weapons. Sometimes, the use of tools and weapons was officially sanctioned as a "good thing" and led to many military campaigns, the birth and collapse of empires and many successive civilizations.

Societies also adopted civil and religious practices to enable reasonably stable coexistence. These laws became the norm and breaking them became a crime. If found, criminals were judged by their peers and punished.

In the mid 1600s, Francis Bacon stated that "Information itself, is power" something which holds true today. The Information Age started – perhaps with the invention of the electric telegraph in 1840. Global networks, such as the telephone and the fax now connect well over one billion people, and the Internet some 400 million.

But can information and information and communications technologies be used as weapons? Certainly, and this book will show the many ways in which human ingenuity has been applied to many forms of crime and to create new forms of warfare.

This book will also explore the current headache that the present legal framework of many countries is only now beginning to address namely, that computer crime and the nature of the offences themselves, do not lend themselves to the gathering of evidence that can be used in a court of law.

2. SETTING THE SCENE FOR INFORMATION SECURITY

Context

The insecurity of computer systems and networks goes much further than the well-known computer viruses, and has now become a priority. This is not paranoia:

Research from the firm Computer Economics estimates that the cost of computer viruses to the U.S. economy in the period January – August 2001 amounts to 10.7 billion dollars, of which 2.6 billion alone can be attributed to the Code Red worm.

In this scenario, what would be the impact on the world economy and stability if (when?) banks, utilities (electricity, water treatment and telecommunications) and air traffic control were to be specifically targeted? Do we need a full-scale information security disaster for this subject to be given the attention it requires?

Information security is not a new topic...

The need to protect information from being seen by people for whom it was not intended, is as old as the history of writing, going back five thousand years or more.

Codes and cyphers have been developed over the centuries as a way to protect information from those not authorised to see it. However ingenious and sophisticated as these methods were, history has shown that sooner or later, all such protection methods were infiltrated and overcome.

In addition, since the beginning of history, crime has been deterred by the prospect of punishment. In the "good old days", such punishment could be dramatic.

Often delegated to the IT department, the protection of information is much more than a technical matter. Human behaviour is just as important and a much more complex topic to manage. Examples include:
- the indiscriminate forwarding of confidential e-mail messages
- the practice of displaying passwords on Post-It™ notes stuck on a computer screen
- parents allowing their children access to their employer's corporate networks from home

- the opening of e-mail attachments known to contain a virus "just to see what they do"

The Information Security Landscape in the Internet Age

Jürgen Storbeck, Director of Europol, recently described the Internet as "a new sphere of life and a new scene of crime".

In the networked world, the new generation of vandals and data thugs do not need to have physical contact with the victim. Data is easily copied, transmitted, modified or destroyed. As a result, the scene of crime is a particularly difficult one: there are no fingerprints or traces, identification of the culprits is nearly impossible, apprehension even more so and the legal framework does not make adequate provision for justice in this kind of crime.

The real-time nature of the Internet adds a further dimension to crime: it's instantaneous. If a thief steals a wallet containing credit cards (with or without the Personal Identification Number or PIN), the thief needs time to use these cards, and the owner has at least a chance to stop the cards before they are used.

When the details of credit cards are stolen from the Internet, the owner does not even know this and the thief, who effectively has stolen a person's electronic identification can, and does, use them immediately.

What is also known about the Internet world is that at the end of 2001 it has some 400 million users and that the number of users, volume of data and volume of traffic continue to increase at a very high rate.

It is projected that by 2004 there will be over 1 billion users on the Internet using fixed and mobile access facilities. Clearly, even a minute percentage of people with malicious intent, constitute a substantial threat.

Many publications suggest that 80% of companies worldwide have suffered malicious software attacks. Cyber-crime, including fraud, is often not reported, but in some countries it has reached the same magnitude as arms and drug trading.

The vulnerability of end users at work, at home and on the move has grown relentlessly. At the same time, dealing with the offenders can no longer be described as looking for a needle in a haystack. We are now looking for a particular needle in a stack of needles, anywhere in the world, often without jurisdiction and without adequate legislation.

Cyberspace: beyond the Internet

When talking about cyberspace, many people think of the World Wide Web. In information security, cyberspace includes the domain of all computer systems connected to networks.

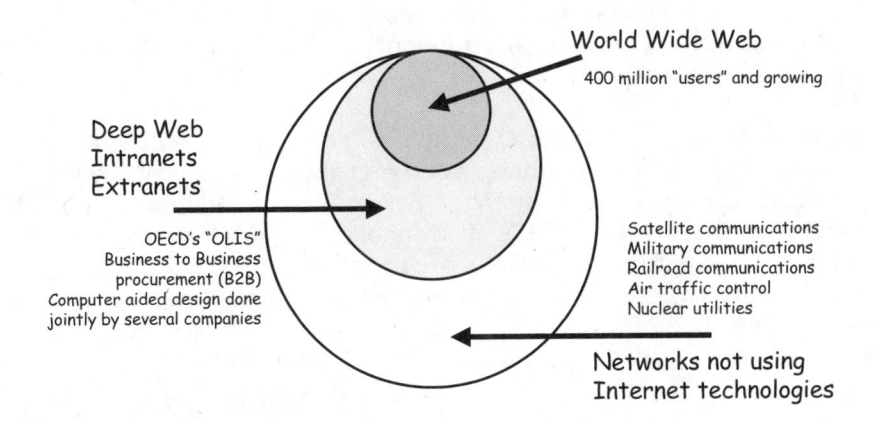

World Wide Web
400 million "users" and growing

Deep Web
Intranets
Extranets

OECD's "OLIS"
Business to Business procurement (B2B)
Computer aided design done jointly by several companies

Satellite communications
Military communications
Railroad communications
Air traffic control
Nuclear utilities

Networks not using Internet technologies

This definition makes cyber-space into a vast domain that, in one way or another, extends into most human activities, only a few of which are shown.

Some of cyberspace's characteristics are explored in a little more detail.

Ownership and governance

Every component part of cyberspace (communications links, satellites, computers, storage devices, data centres, telephone exchanges, etc) has an identifiable owner. The same is true for the data that flows around cyberspace.

This is no different from marine transportation: all ports and their facilities have owners, and so do all ships. Each item of cargo on a ship also has an owner. There is one difference however: the international community developed and adopted the Law of the Seas.

The Law of the Seas defines all aspects of the uses of the seas, including civilian, commercial and military navigation, continental shelves, island and archipelago states, the concept of the "high seas", conservation and management of species living in the seas, the common heritage of mankind, governance and many other topics.

There is no equivalent for cyberspace. The current governance of cyberspace is divided among many groups, some composed of volunteers such as the Internet Engineering Task Force (IETF), some like the World Wide Web Consortium (W3C) or the ICANN, composed and funded by 500 private and public sector entities, others run by the private sector, as are many domain name registration bodies.

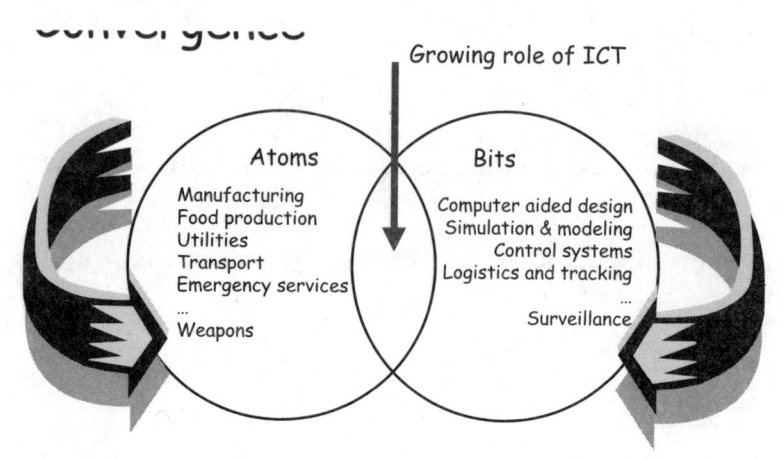

Growing role of ICT

Atoms
Manufacturing
Food production
Utilities
Transport
Emergency services
...
Weapons

Bits
Computer aided design
Simulation & modeling
Control systems
Logistics and tracking
...
Surveillance

In 2002, International Organisations play a relatively peripheral role in cyberspace dealing with certain aspects of e-commerce (UNCTAD and WTO), intellectual property (WIPO), and technical standards (ITU, ISO and IEC).

Other efforts to put into place appropriate governance and legislative mechanisms for cyber-space remain fragmented and include initiatives such as the Council of Europe's Convention on Cyber-crime issued in 2001 and various national and regional Data Protection laws, but not yet at the truly global level.

Convergence

In the history of human evolution, the world of atoms – the world of physical objects – dominated until the second half of the 20th Century.

As we learned to work with binary logic and data, this allowed the automation of repetitive processes, initially in payroll and accounting offices, financial services and other "information rich" activities.

Binary formats started to be used in networks and other telecommunications links (such as satellites) many years ago.

The technologies for photocopying, imaging and digitalising music were developed in the 1960s and matured quickly.

Personal computers (PC) have been around since the mid 1970s and the adoption of the 16-bit PC as a "personal productivity" tool in the early 1980s caused a revolution. The Internet has also existed for more than 30 years and the World Wide Web for more than 10 years but they became visible to the world at large around 1994 when the MOSAIC browser with its easy to use interface to access information became available.

Today, there are few activities in the developed world that do not use information technologies and are not connected to some kind of network. This is why security has become an issue.

What makes cyber-attacks special

Computer crime has existed at least as long as computers. In the early days knowledgeable insiders carried out computer crime, as the expertise required was limited to "mathematical geniuses".

Those smart enough not to draw attention to themselves performed fraudulent transactions for a long time, often without being discovered. Others, not worried about identifying themselves, planted malicious code such as a logical bomb to extort payment.

This kind of insider attacks continues. As the workforce has growing computer skills, having knowledge, legitimate access and motive makes it easier for insiders to commit computer crime.

The situation is made worse by the unwillingness of organizations to disclose that they have been targeted. Even when offenders are identified and evidence acceptable to a court of law is available, prosecution is rare.

The emergence of the Internet with its outreach to some 400 million plus cybernauts has widened the potential for mischief.

Easy to learn techniques and acquire tools

Many network operators and countries may be involved

Small investment can cause massive economic damage

No need for physical contact with the victims

When done subtly it leaves few or no traces

Easy for the players to hide

Inadequate cyberspace legislation

Whenever a hacker is traced, it is as a result of a massive, long and complex coordinated search. Many countries do not have the legislation to prosecute cyber-offenders. There have been several instances of people being arrested and subsequently released without charge (the author of the "I Love You" virus in the Philippines) or with minimal penalties (the author of the "Anna Kournikova" virus in the Netherlands).

3. INFORMATION SECURITY PRINCIPLES

What exactly is Information Security?

Basically, it is the discipline that addresses all the issues involving the protection of data and information in all forms, the related technologies used for information processing, storage and communications, and the computer resources of an individual or an organization.

Information has three characteristics: it has substance, it can be recorded and retrieved and it has value. It can exist in many forms, e.g. written, printed, spoken, electronically stored, physically transmitted or transmitted in electronic form. It can be created, processed, used, stored, transmitted, corrupted, lost and destroyed.

The formal definition of information security relies on two sets of parameters:
- Threats, Vulnerability, Assets and Residual risk
- Availability, Integrity and Confidentiality

Information security has many technical components, it depends on human behaviour and it is influenced by the presence of many players: management, staff, internal and external auditors, legal counsel, external interested parties and stakeholders. There are also those motivated to breach an organization's defences to access data and information.

Asset

An asset is anything to which an individual or an organization assigns value. Of specific relevance to information security, all of the following fall into the category of "asset": documents, data, databases, software, physical information technology assets (computers, networks, etc), proprietary processes, industry specific exclusive knowledge, reputation and image. The valuation of such assets constitutes an essential part of any approach to information security.

Residual Risk

For a given set of assets, vulnerabilities and threats, it is possible to assess the risk that these assets will be damaged or compromised.

This is not unique to information: it is possible to design a building so that it can withstand an earthquake. The cost of doing so increases rapidly with the severity of the earthquake it should be able to survive.

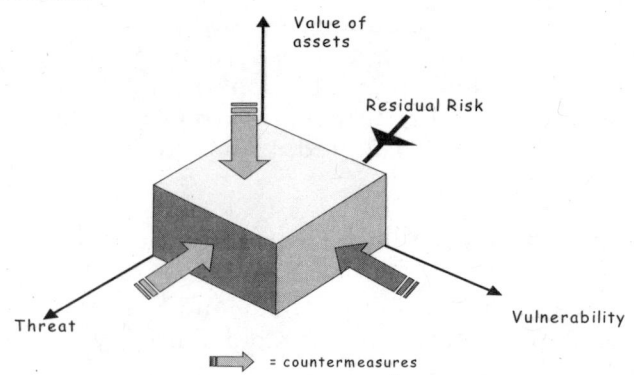

The compromise between cost and survivability implies the acceptance of a residual risk.

Organizations operating critical infrastructures, as well as military, policy and emergency services would normally accept the lowest level of residual risk. Banks, airlines and major outsourcing service providers may be able to accept a slightly higher level or residual risk. Low-tech manufacturing would be expected to have a greater tolerance to risk than any of the above organizations.

Availability

This is defined as the property of a system (or of a specific system resource) to be accessible and usable whenever required by an authorised entity and according to performance specifications appropriate to the system.

Availability is usually expressed as a percentage, interpreted as follows:
- 99.9% implies that a system will operate as expected other than for a total of approximately 8 hours in a year. The non-operational time excludes *planned* outages.
- 99.99% implies that the cumulative non-operational time does not exceed 50 minutes in a year
- 99.999% implies that the cumulative non-operational time does not exceed 5 minutes in a year

Systems and facilities operating seven days a week, 24 hours a day, can achieve such availability targets – at a cost. Cost increases at a faster rate than availability gains, and so do the resources needed to manage it and the complexity of the facilities.

Integrity

This is defined as the property that data has not been changed, destroyed or lost in an unauthorised or accidental manner.

In practice, there are additional aspects to integrity, dealing with the confidence in data values and the information these values represent (correctness integrity) and with the trustworthiness of the source of the values (source integrity).

Attacks on the integrity of information can have as an objective fraud (e.g. falsifying the records in a payroll system) or a political motive (e.g. modifying the contents of a website).

Confidentiality

This is defined as the property that information (or data) is not made available or disclosed to unauthorised individuals, entities or processes.

Techniques, such as encryption, are used to obscure the contents of information and data from parties who do not have access to decryption facilities.

The three principles of Information Security

Principle N° 1: 100% security is unachievable

For every security system and device there is at least one way to bypass it. The knowledge of how this is done used to be restricted to very few people and not disclosed. In cyberspace this is no longer the case. In the context of Information Security, it is accepted throughout the industry that:
- Whilst software is designed to perform specific functions, experts – and these include hackers and crackers – can make it do other things
- Perfect software does not exist – all software contains bugs – coding errors in computer programs.

Moreover, a substantial amount of software includes features that were not part of the design specification and in practice software is only tested to confirm that it performs the functions specified. It is rarely tested to identify if it performs other – unwanted – functions. Such functions may include back doors, logic bombs and unauthorised special access rights to specific individuals.

In addition, in recent years, desktop software often includes hidden programs (referred to as "Easter Eggs" by the people who include such features), which range from games to the list of the names of the software designers.

The same is true for the management of information security – however good the procedures and practices applied, these may contain gaps, may be the subject of human error or the target of malicious intent.

In practice all of the following four statements are true:
- New software means new bugs
- Old bugs are not always fixed
- Fixes are not always installed
- Fixes may contain new bugs

The result is that you only find out how effective your information security is when a security incident occurs, and then only if it is detected! Organizations that handle information security proactively will often engage security auditors to carry out unannounced tests to determine if they can breach the defenses in place. Otherwise, the security incident will be caused by someone who has different motives.

Once a security incident has taken place, it may be possible to identify weaknesses in the arrangements, investigate and repair them.

The biggest challenge of information security is that of overcoming an organization's "comfort zone": the belief that their arrangements are adequate because a security incident has not occurred in the past or has not been detected.

Statements such as "we have a firewall ", "we use a 128 bit encryption key", etc. are, by themselves, no substitute for a set of robust security policies, tools, measures, controls and a determined approach to compliance.

Principle N° 2: Risk and expenditure need to be balanced

We all take measures to protect our property and ourselves.

The degree to which we implement such measures is influenced by our assessment of potential risks and our willingness to accept the restrictions and the constraints that such measures will impose on our daily life and their cost.

We need to recognise however that in real life:
- Whatever protective measures we take, there is no guarantee that they will be <u>totally</u> effective <u>all</u> the time
- The risks against which we seek to protect ourselves will change in time and the assessment process and protective measures taken need to change accordingly to be effective
- Security measures involve investments and recurrent expenditures. Both of these could be significant

A fundamental component of the practice of information security is the assessment of the value of the assets to be protected, the threats and vulnerabilities to which they may be subject and the impact that a security breach could have.

Finally, as in the case of household insurance, it is necessary to define the level of residual risk that can be accepted.

<u>Principle N° 3: Security and inconvenience need to be balanced</u>

In the world of security nothing is perfect. This is true for information as well as for the protection of our property and person.

Every security measure added implies an additional process or activity to end-users. As these measures add up, they become obstacles to be overcome by each end user, regardless of whether they are multiple locks and burglar alarms or the need to remember several passwords. The workload of the Systems Administrator also increases as a result.

Human nature is such that people will look for shortcuts to complex processes. It is not unusual for multiple or complex passwords to be written down. Worse still, these can be found on a Post-It™ note affixed in a visible place. This weakens, if not altogether invalidates, the whole security process.

Inventories
Insurance

Strong locks
Burglar alarm
Remote monitoring
Reinforced doors
Impact resisting glass
CCTV

4. THE INFORMATION SECURITY PLAYERS

The medieval battleground

Medieval sieges and battles, as related in history books, appear to have many similarities with today's information security attacks. There are many different forms of attack – just as there were many forms of weapons. The difference lies in the fact that today's weapons become more sophisticated very quickly.

There are many kinds of warriors – from the leader and the professional soldier to the mercenaries and peasants conscripted against their will. Today's players also include professionals such as mercenaries who hack for personal gain or satisfaction; and those who hijack computers and turn them into zombies by planting them with malicious software. On the side of the defenders we may find "reformed hackers" who become security advisors and consultants.

As the various components of information technology (computers, networks and software) became tools, they took three roles in information security:
- Tools to perpetrate information offences
- Weapons
- Target for attack

The role of <u>target</u> for an attack is the oldest and best established and will be discussed later in this book when dealing the various kinds of "bad guys". Typical offences against a computer system include fraud, extortion, denial of service and the theft of proprietary information, either as the result of espionage or with intent to misuse it as for example credit cards details.

The use of information technology as a tool or accessory also has a long history, which begins in World War II when early computers were used to break down codes used to encrypt military communications.

The use of information technology as a weapon is most evident when combined with other kind of weapons such as missiles, to provide them with additional capabilities such as the identification of targets and enhanced navigation. Malicious code, software designed to perform functions which will interfere with the operation of a computer or network, such as virus and worm software, are the latest manifestation of "weapons" of considerable economic impact.

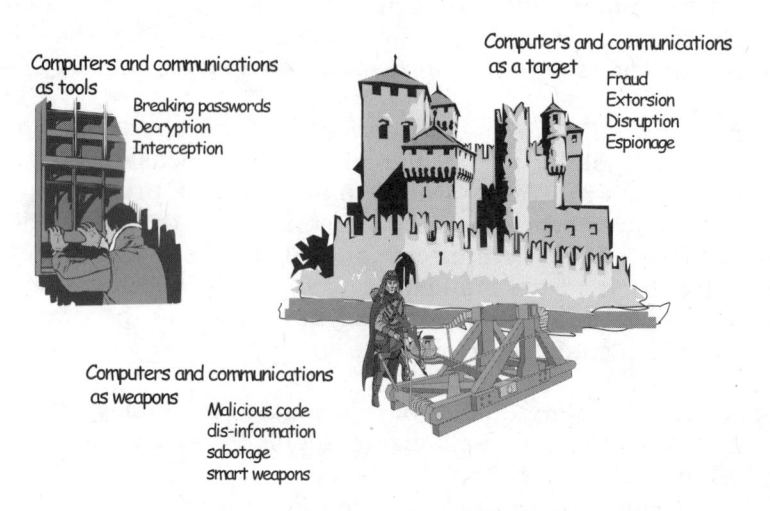

Computers and communications as tools
- Breaking passwords
- Decryption
- Interception

Computers and communications as a target
- Fraud
- Extorsion
- Disruption
- Espionage

Computers and communications as weapons
- Malicious code
- dis-information
- sabotage
- smart weapons

Here are some numbers that illustrate the potential cost of information **in**security:

In the year 2000, the U.S. Association of Certified Fraud Examiners reported that the average sum of money robbed in a bank holdup was 14,000 dollars whereas the average computer theft was 2 million dollars.

Early in 2002, Computer Economics Inc., a U.S. company reported that their estimate for the total cost of computer virus and worm attacks to the U.S. economy amounted to 17 billion dollars. This estimate assumes that the average cost of an employee doing computer work in the U.S.A. is one dollar per minute and that the economic impact from malicious code includes the cost of:
- Removing all malicious code from computers and servers
- Restoring lost and corrupted data
- Returning all systems to normal operations
- Providing support to end-users, customers and other parties involved
- Lost productivity while the above processes took place

This economic impact needs to be seen in the context that:
- Computer systems are becoming more complex and, as a result, have greater vulnerabilities than previous generations – effectively doubling every year
- The trend for malicious code attacks shows a similar increase also doubling every year

This can be seen from the tables below, produced by the Carnegie-Mellon University Computer Emergency Response Team (CERT), a leading centre for providing alerts and guidance on malicious code.

Vulnerabilities reported to CERT

Year	1995	1996	1997	1998	1999	2000	2001
Vulnerabilities	171	345	311	262	417	1090	2437

Number of incidents reported to CERT

Year	1988	1989	1990	1991	1992	1993	1994
Incidents reported	6	132	252	406	773	1334	2340

Year	1995	1996	1997	1998	1999	2000	2001
Incidents reported	2402	2573	2134	3734	9859	21756	52658

These figures are roughly doubling every year in number. The sophistication of the tools and methods to create incidents is also growing fast.

Today's "threatscape"

This differs from that of medieval times for three main reasons:
- The timeframe has changed. Everything happens very quickly. In the middle ages, a good catapult team could shoot no more than two stones an hour.
- Physical security has become less dominant than logical security – data thugs, cyber-vandals and other players do not need physical contact with the victim.
- There is no need any longer to physically manufacture and transport weapons.

Today's information security players

This section discusses these players in two categories: by nature and by function. It also discusses, to the extent possible, what may motivate them.

Information security players by nature

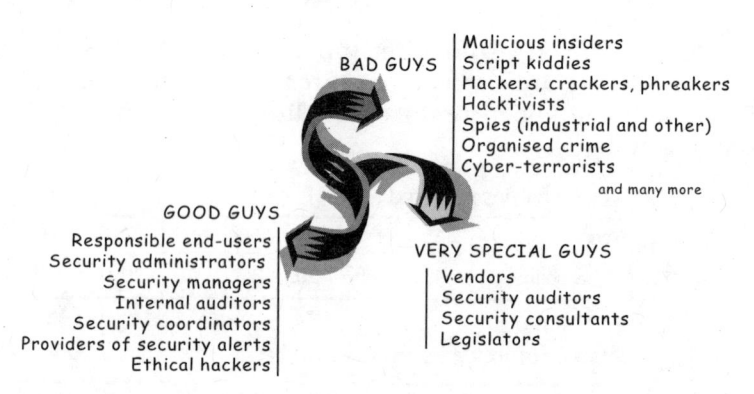

```
                                    Malicious insiders
                         BAD GUYS   Script kiddies
                                    Hackers, crackers, phreakers
                                    Hacktivists
                                    Spies (industrial and other)
                                    Organised crime
                                    Cyber-terrorists
                                                    and many more
              GOOD GUYS
         Responsible end-users
         Security administrators    VERY SPECIAL GUYS
            Security managers       Vendors
             Internal auditors      Security auditors
          Security coordinators     Security consultants
      Providers of security alerts  Legislators
              Ethical hackers
```

Good Guys can be described in just a few lines: these are the people whose role is to protect themselves and their employers from all forms of cyber-attack. How they actually do this is the subject of Information Security Management, a topic covered by extensive, largely technical bibliography and several professional journals and websites.

These players are motivated by their work ethics to behave ethically, in the best interest of their employers and by deriving a high degree of job satisfaction.

Ethical hackers deserve a special mention: these are people with good technical knowledge and an understanding of how to identify vulnerabilities in products and procedures, and how to do so with the purpose of alerting their employer, vendors and bodies that monitor product vulnerabilities. The best ethical hackers often become professional security consultants and conduct controlled tests for organisations.

Very Special Guys are those external people who play key roles in defining security. Among them, vendors have the responsibility of providing products with the least possible number of vulnerabilities.

This may be incompatible with the commercial pressures to bring products to market ahead of potential competitors and to generate new revenues. It is important to note that many software vendors disclaim liabilities for weaknesses, vulnerabilities or errors in their products whatever consequences these may cause to the end-user.

When engaging security auditors there needs to be a very strong measure of trust as they will examine in detail and test security arrangements. Through this process they will acquire highly sensitive knowledge.

Bad Guys are those players whose intent is to interfere with someone else's computer systems and data.

```
                    Access
        ┌─────────────────────────┐
        │   Malicious insiders    │
        │     Script kiddies      │
        │ Hackers, crackers, phreakers │
        │       Hacktivists       │
        │ Spies (industrial and other) │
        │     Organised crime     │
        │     Cyber-terrorists    │
        └─────────────────────────┘
  Knowledge                      Motivation
```

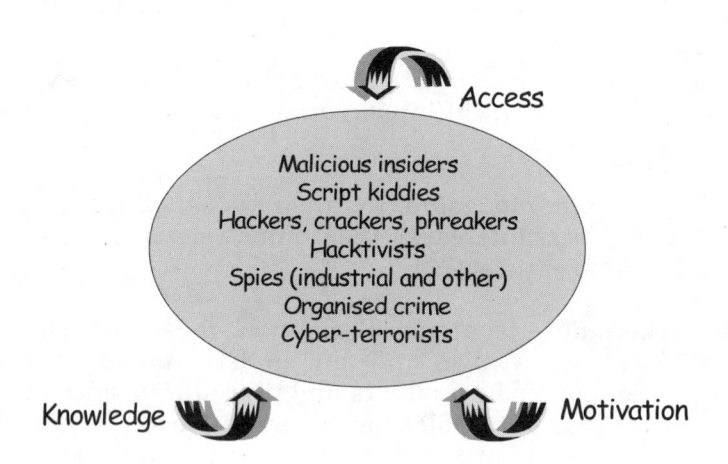

Malicious insiders

Any review of the Bad Guys must start with them. They are the most likely to combine access, knowledge and motivation to act against computer data, systems and networks. Motivation usually falls into two categories:
1. Those who seek financial gain for themselves and/or close associates by defrauding or extorting their employer. Computer fraud involves large sums of money, no physical violence and when done subtly, a good chance to remain undetected. Even when detected, it is difficult to produce evidence that will satisfy a court of law. Computer crimes leave few or no traces, there are unlikely to be witnesses and, given the risk to an organisation's reputation, such crimes are usually unreported.
2. Those driven to cause damage as a result of grudges against their employers or their colleagues, being coerced by a third party or in support of a political cause. These are, by far the most dangerous. Insiders know the vulnerabilities of systems and can corrupt data and software, plant malicious code, or sabotage their employers' systems in many other ways.

The situation where a malicious insider who works for a country's critical infrastructures behaves as a cyber-terrorist, represents the most serious risk. It also presents an ethical dilemma for employers, that of closely monitoring the activities of their employees and ensuring compliance with security policies.

Script-kiddies

These are usually young people who like computers but are not particularly knowledgeable. By visiting hacker club websites, chat-rooms and exchanging readily available tools with their peers, they can emulate more knowledgeable players. They tend to be motivated to emulate the exploits of knowledgeable hackers.

Hackers, crackers and other

Hackers are technically knowledgeable people who understand and write software, and know how to identify security weaknesses in products. This enables them to make other peoples' software perform undesired functions, as well as to create tools to facilitate their exploits.

Hacker groups are well organised to share knowledge, certainly better than security managers: They convene conferences, run good websites, exchange tools and information on product weaknesses (without reporting them to the product vendors). The annual DEFCON conference describes itself as the "largest underground internet security gathering on the planet" and is a public event. The first DEFCON conference took place in 1993.

Ethical hackers appear to be happy being able to prove they can overcome someone else's security defences. In a way they can be thought of as "explorers" trying to map a new, uncharted territory. Unethical hackers do so with intent to causing damage, or at the very least, embarrassment. Instead of explorers, they are like pirates and mercenaries and equally outside the law (where such laws exist).

International Organisations (such as the World Trade Organisation) and commercial companies have been the subject of synchronised Distributed Denial of Service attacks, in which their web servers and e-mail servers are bombarded by transactions to the point that they become unable to operate.

These attacks make use of computers hijacked without their owners' knowledge by planting software in them that turns them into "zombies" whenever the hackers need them.

Whenever hackers give interviews or write articles, they say little about their motivation. The reasons most frequently given by non-ethical hackers are:
- "Just because it's there and I know how to"
- "To cause maximum inconvenience and embarrassment"
- "To have access to data which allows fraudulent transactions to take place"

Writers of malicious code

"Malicious code" is an umbrella term for any computer software designed to make computers perform unwanted actions. Two best known forms of malicious code are **viruses** and **worms**. (Viruses use software in the affected machine to replicate. Worms are self-replicating).

Other forms of malicious code include:
- Macros written for Microsoft Office applications (file extension .vbs). This was used in the Melissa virus
- Executable files (file extension .exe). A recent virus was hidden in a digital picture file (file extension .jpeg). This technique is called steganography.
- Trojan Horse – software which performs legitimate functions but which includes within it malicious code

The skills and tools needed to write and/or modify viruses and worms are within the grasp of anyone with reasonable programming skills. Most of them are short programs and many are variants of a previous one. The producers of Anti-Virus software to develop the tools to detect and eliminate them use their "signature", like the DNA of biological viruses. Usually the detection software becomes available only after the code has infected a large number of machines.

It is not clear what motivates writers of malicious code. Some have no more than a perverse desire to indulge in a "practical joke". Others may be sponsored by other parties to research and develop mechanisms to access computers that evade detection for long enough to cause damage. The emergence of a military-strength virus with a destructive payload that can corrupt or delete data and programs is inevitable and simply a matter of time.

Other forms of malicious code have been in existence since early computer applications, in this case designed and introduced by expert programmers. Examples of such code include:
- Logic bomb
- Back door and/or unauthorised Super-user rights
- Fraudulent transactions

A <u>logical bomb</u> is a piece of software which is concealed within an application, and which can be activated by its designer. An example is when the person has a grudge against the company where the software has been planted. Alternatively, the objective may be extortion or blackmail. Once activated, the usual script is as follows:
- Your payroll system will grind to a halt.
- I'm the only person who knows how to prevent it.
- If you wanted fixed, it will cost you....

A logical bomb is, in reality, "extra code", software that was never part of a system's specification. Finding and removing such code is easier said than done as some software consists of millions of line of code and the quality of source-code documentation is variable.

In the case of packaged software (such as a commercial product), the source code is not available for inspection and it is known that the practice of including extra code is regularly practiced. Non-malicious extra code, referred to as "Easter Eggs" is usually well hidden and may consist of games, the list of names of the software design team, utilities, etc.

Disabling all extra code and software features, which are not specifically needed, is always a good security practice. This is easier said than done.

Back door and/or Super-user access rights are hidden in a system by designers to bypass security features and access data and the programs without having the authority to do so. Even with extensive auditing of computer systems, such back doors usually remain undiscovered given the size and complexity of such applications.

The people who introduce such features have malicious intent against their employer, a target organization. This could be used for sabotage, extortion or to financially benefit the writer.

Hacktivists

The World Wide Web and Internet mail have enabled political activism to take new forms, such as Electronic Sit-Ins, the defacement of websites, or the hijacking of websites by redirecting traffic to a spoof website.

The hacktivists' targets are usually government websites, international and multinational organizations, financial institutions. Hacktivists claim that this is a form of civil disobedience. The legal status of these actions is unclear in existing legislation.

Hacktivists have been highly successful in some recent civil disobedience actions.

Hacktivists claim that cyberspace gives them opportunity to make themselves heard on a global scale and gain publicity for the causes they support. A different form of hacktivism is the use of cyberspace to disseminate propaganda, disinformation, and incitation to violence and hate.

Spies (industrial and other)

Espionage has a long history. Ever since the industrial revolution, industrial espionage has been big business, particularly where achieving and maintaining a position of leadership in a competitive market requires sophisticated research. Industrial espionage is on the increase because of the extensive reliance on computer systems and networks to document experiments and research. It is motivated by money – it is a well paid activity and the sponsor stands to gain knowledge worth millions of dollars at minimal expense and minimal risk.

The gathering of military and other intelligence is no longer exclusive to governments: it is also practiced by organised crime, guerrillas and terrorists.

Electronic surveillance is practiced worldwide and the degree to which the existence of surveillance systems is reported in the press varies. Some systems are acknowledged: FBI's "Carnivore" is now called DCS1000. Others, despite rumours, may or may not exist such as "Echelon", the surveillance network supposed to have been set up by a number of governments to monitor global information flows.

An e-mail message is no more than a machine-readable unsealed postcard. Whilst the use of foreign languages and/or encryption for such messages provides a measure of assurance of confidentiality, it also signals to scanning systems (likely to exist despite denials) that the writer wants to keep something hidden. Encrypted messages become the focus of even greater attention.

Organised crime

Technological innovations are quickly exploited by organized criminals for personal gain. Information and communication technologies are no different, and new forms of fraudulent and anti-social activities continue to emerge. It is invariably motivated by money, in most cases tax-free.

Current examples include the use of cyberspace for money laundering, credit card fraud, blackmail, extortion, pornography, pedophilia, and offshore gambling. Most of these activities are aided by the ease of hiding in cyberspace, the lack of jurisdiction over cyberspace and the number of countries that do not have adequate legislation to address such activities. Even when the legislation exists, enforcing it may be a very complex matter.

Cyber-terrorists and cyber-warriors

There appears to be no agreed definition of a cyber-terrorist or of what constitutes "violence" in cyber-space. The latter is likely to become a subject of some concern in future as the gap between levels of technology advances further.

Some of the recent manifestations of worms such as CODE RED in the Summer of 2001 and the NIMDA worm, may be a proof of concept for software that could paralyse the Internet and organisations that rely on it for their operations.

The potential impact of a well-conducted cyber-attack in which the most likely targets would be critical infrastructures could be the equivalent of a full scale cyber-war.

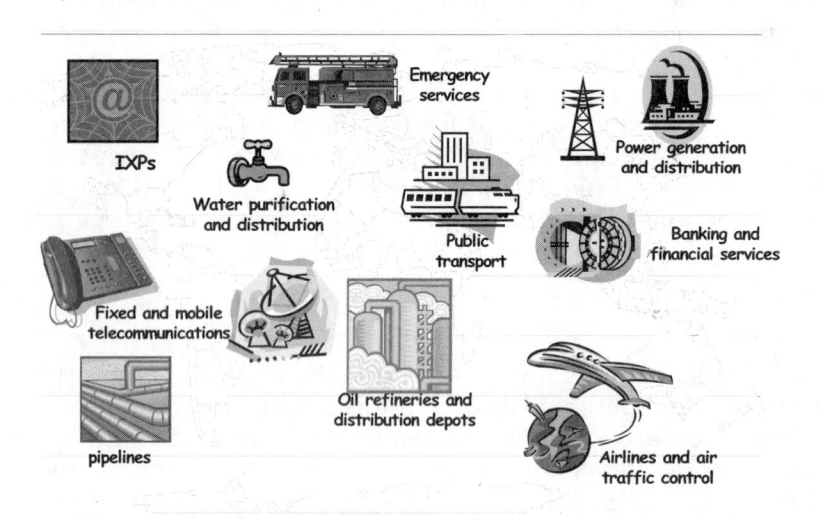

IXPs
Water purification and distribution
Emergency services
Public transport
Power generation and distribution
Banking and financial services
Fixed and mobile telecommunications
Oil refineries and distribution depots
pipelines
Airlines and air traffic control

Information Security players by organisation

Critical Infrastructures

In the developed world, there are a large number of services and facilities that have become essential to what is thought of as "normal life". Most of them are obvious, such as utilities, financial and emergency services and public transport. Some are less so, such as is the case of Internet Exchange Points – a hundred or so places around the world where Internet Service Providers interconnect.

Wherever society has a culture of openness and transparency, much information about these critical infrastructures is readily available often online. The exact physical location of many Internet Exchange Points is in the public domain and this makes the work of security personnel that much more difficult.

Because of their important role in the functioning of an orderly society, security managers working in critical infrastructures have to accept many special responsibilities:
- Their computing, networking, systems and facilities must be highly secure
- They must continually monitor for vulnerabilities and attacks
- They must have in place an Emergency Response Team and well developed and tested procedures to deal with security incidents
- They must have proven and tested disaster recovery, business continuity and crisis management plans and processes
- They must have an adequate number of trusted, qualified and trained security personnel
- Their interfaces with the public Internet must be sufficiently secure
- They should seek, achieve and maintain security certification
- They must maintain effective co-ordination with other critical infrastructures and exchange information on a regular basis

The work of providing information security for critical infrastructures requires an appropriate government framework.

National government and legislation

Regardless of the ownership of the critical infrastructures, governments should implement national information security programs and ensure that regular information security audits are conducted for critical infrastructures and key functions of government agencies.

It is also important that national governments should promote and adopt international standards and promote best practices for information security.

All of the responsibilities listed above for critical infrastructures should also apply, to the appropriate degree, to government agencies and these should also conduct information security awareness training for all personnel.

International Organisations

There is much to be done by International Organisations to strengthen information security worldwide. In particular:
- Encourage the development and adoption of international standards, regardless if these are de-jure or de-facto
- Develop appropriate mechanism for international cooperation including a framework that avoids the possibility of "islands" in cyberspace where organised crime and cyber-terrorists can legally exist
- Establish effective cyberspace governance mechanisms
- Create effective fora for the sharing of information on information security

The value of such cooperation was already proven by the two meetings of National Y2K Coordinators that took place in New York in 1998 and 1999 under the auspices of the United Nations.

Vendors and service providers

In the perfect world, vendors and service providers would exercise a higher level of quality assurance and security validation than appears to be the case at present. Many vendors product release policies appear to be driven by an urgency to be first in the marketplace and/or to release "fatware" loaded with functionality, with new versions succeeding each other at frequent short intervals.

The commercial incentives for doing so are understandable, but this results in buggy software and endless stream of "patches", "service packs", vulnerability alerts and downloads which present a major challenge to network administrators and to individuals.

A detailed examination of the terms and conditions of many software licenses reveals that vendors do not accept liability for any defects that the software may have.

Service providers, particularly ISPs, have a major role to play in tracking bad guys as their logs will enable the identification of sources and flows as well as access to copies of transactions.

However, other service providers, such as the anonymous remailers, work against such practices and instead provide useful tools for organised crime and cyber-terrorists. The international community faces the challenge that one or more countries may choose to stay outside agreements on the types of services and facilities that should be available in cyberspace. This can provide a valuable hiding place for uncivil society.

Academic Institutions

Characterised by a tradition of academic freedom, many attacks and malicious software designs have been traced as having originated in academic institutions. Their governing bodies have a responsibility to ensure that the ethical aspects of cyberspace are understood and respected.

Businesses, organisations and individual users

Their responsibilities are essentially internal and require that information security be managed in a manner consistent with the value of their information assets.

Unaware insiders

These are the employees, temporary staff, contractors, consultants and others working in an organization and granted various levels of system and network access rights who are unaware of the organization's security policies and practices and possibly genuinely not knowledgeable about information security issues.

Under these circumstances, they may leave their passwords prominently displayed on a computer screen, open attachments containing malicious software which managed to get through the organization's defences, download shareware and freeware from websites, bring infected floppy disks or CD-ROMs into the organization, etc.

Security managers and administrators

These are the individuals whose responsibility it is to define, maintain and monitor an organizations defences against malicious code and the misuse of computer systems and networks.

By 2001, this has become a major job, with considerable responsibilities, requiring close contact with all parts of an organization.

Security Consultants

The growing complexity of this field has led to the development of a major new service: consultancy in information systems security.

Such consultancy services can include the development of security policies, conducting security awareness seminars, highly detailed technical reviews of products and how these are configured and applied, the development of best practices in the monitoring and resolution of security incidents, etc.

Auditors

Two distinct types of security audits need to be considered: Compliance and Penetration audits.

Compliance audits focus on the way in which security policies and practices are applied in an organization, how they are monitored, how incidents are dealt with and how effective they are.

Penetration audits involve creating a controlled attack on the organization's security arrangements, with or without prior warning. The purpose of these tests is to identify weaknesses in the defences and the subsequent development of recommendations for corrective action.

Whenever an external company is used for such security audits, reliable references are essential as you will be revealing to them all the details of your security arrangements, technologies, organization, etc.

5. HIDING IN CYBERSPACE

The ease with which it is possible to hide in cyberspace – nobody knows who you are or where you are located – gives the "bad guys" a considerable advantage.

There are two complementary ways of hiding in cyberspace: hiding information and becoming anonymous.

The discipline of Digital Forensics deals with finding information hidden in cyberspace and turning it into evidence acceptable to a court of law.

Hiding information

There are many ways to hide information in digital form. The five most common are: hidden files, file compression, steganography, password protection of files, directories and computers and encryption.

Hidden files can be easily placed in a personal computer in different ways. Windows has a category of files – "hidden files" which are not displayed when examining a directory. Other ways to hide files include renaming it as a "temporary file" and placing it in a temporary folder. The owner of the file can easily retrieve it but a forensic investigator would need to examine all temporary files, which could be in the hundreds.

Compression involves reducing the size file by using an algorithm that allows this function and its subsequent simple reversal (WinZip is a product that performs this function). Custom designed compression algorithms can be hard to break without knowing what approach the designer took. The file is visible in the directory but, having been compressed it may be impossible to determine what program was used to create it or how to decompress it.

Steganography is one of many techniques for embedding information into another file so that it is hidden. The Anna Kournikova virus consisted of code embedded in a .jpeg file with an image of the tennis player. Steganography software is easily obtained or written.

Passwords are one of the oldest methods for preventing third parties from opening a file, directory or computer. There are several password breaking tools available from the hacker community that will break even a well designed password that contains mixed capitals and lower case characters, as well as a mixture of alpha and numeric characters. Given enough effort and time no passwords are break-proof.

Encryption transforms intelligible information into a format that can only be recovered if the key to the code is available. This technique has been used since the invention of writing. While it is theoretically possible to break a code that is based on mathematical processes, this usually requires considerable computing power and time.

Should the code be based on a different approach, such as a one time code based on a particular book, it cannot be easily broken without the full knowledge of the code.

Anonymity

Anonymous remailers are mechanisms that allow e-mail to be sent in a way that does not identify the sender who cannot then be traced or identified. Anonymous remailer services can be linked in a chain to make it even harder to trace a message. Messages are typically encrypted.

Type-II or Mixmaster remailers, now the most commonly used, fragments messages into fixed-size packets that makes traffic analysis hard. This type of remailer requires the user to have special client software (typically Mixmaster or JBN).

Anonymous browsing is a facility available for a small fee from several sources. It masks the user's IP address and provides additional facilities such as cookie management, which allows a person to surf the Internet without leaving a trace of physical location, identity or Internet Service Provider.

Computer penetration and looping are techniques used by hackers to penetrate a network and gain control of an end-user's computer. Sophisticated hackers have developed techniques such as "distributed metastasis" that use agents to increase the depth of network penetration.

Cell-phone cloning occurs when hackers have made a copy of a valid SIM card and create a clone of a legitimate account to intercept phone calls, to listen to conversations and acquire personal information such as credit card details. It can also be used to make calls anonymously as they are registered and charged to a proper account without the possibility of locating the cloned copy.

Cell-phone prepaid cards are the mobile equivalent of the coin operated public telephone. This allows an individual to make call totally anonymously from a rented cell-phone with minimal or zero possibility of tracking, tapping or subsequent tracing of the call.

Digital forensics

Digital forensics is the extension of the techniques used in audit and police investigations to the world of bits. It will gain in importance as information security is recognised as a threat to commercial companies, government departments and individuals.

The essence of digital forensics is the acquisition, safeguarding and analysis of computer data in such a way that the findings can be used in a court of law as evidence.

"e-Evidence" presents three distinct headaches:
- It is difficult to acquire and preserve, particularly when the attack originated in another country.
- Losses are hard to quantify (except for financial fraud).
- It is unclear what may or may not be admissible in a court of law.

The nature of the offence will determine whether any prosecution will take place in a civil court or in a criminal court. It needs to be noted however, that many organizations will not publicise information security breaches as this may have a serious impact on their reputation and stock market valuation. Financial fraud offences are usually settled out of court.

Another potential legal scenario is when the IT Manager or Chief Information Officer is taken to court to determine whether there was due diligence on her/his part, negligence, dereliction of duty, misconduct, sabotage or aiding and abetting organized crime or terrorism. In many of these cases, the minimum penalty is dismissal.

6. Information Security Offences

This section is not comprehensive. It merely describes the nature of the most common form of attacks on information systems grouped in four categories of offences:
- Network-related
- Data-related
- Access-related
- Computer-related

All four forms impact deeply on the objectives of the organisation owning the information system.

Network related offences

These can be subdivided into three categories: interference, sabotage and anonymity

Interference

The most common techniques for interfering with a network are Denial of Service Attacks, using a trusted network to gain access to another computer or network, "sniffing" traffic and hoaxes and brute force entry into a network.

Denial of Service and Distributed Denial of Service

The techniques used to overwhelm the corporate systems – until now websites and e-mail servers – by arranging to deliver massive pings, requests for web pages or thousands of e-mail messages in a very short period of time.

These can be driven by a group of people acting in concert, as was the case when in 1999 cyber-hippies who organised a Distributed Denial of Service attack on the website of the World Trade Organization relied on cooperation amongst like-minded individuals to share software that could launch such an attack. More recently, these attacks have been automated by using someone else's computer without their knowledge.

Hijacking of an end-user's personal computer

Recent developments have automated the process of infiltrating an end-user's computer, to turn it on demand into a Zombie or a slave computer that will then perform whatever tasks the worm is designed to make it perform.

Such a Zombie could also be programmed to provide a back door into a corporate network thus bypassing all security measures designed to keep outsiders out. Recent Internet worms such as Code Red and Nimda could be used for this purpose and/or carry a destructive payload that could affect data and programs.

Spoofing and redirection of traffic

This is done either to impersonate a legitimate user or to redirect traffic to another location that contains content that has been modified without the knowledge of the original owner of the site.

This modified content may be used to steal credit card details, to discredit the original owner or to provide disinformation or propaganda.

Current legislation does not usually allow for the prosecution of a person impersonating someone else online.

Hoaxes

A fake attack that causes network and systems administrators considerable waste of time and can, when done properly, demand an in-depth investigation of a network and all the devices connected to it. It is the equivalent of a false alarm that then creates the need for a voluntary stoppage of the system.

Computer network break-in (brute force access)

Hackers can break into computer systems using tools they have developed, procured or downloaded free from the Internet. Once inside someone else's computer or network, hackers can steal data, including legitimate passwords, plant malicious code or simply cause chaos by modifying corporate data, website pages, etc.

Network intrusions of this kind are, when carried out by a serious hacker, difficult to detect. Even when detected, the identification of the culprit, who is often in another location, and possibly in another country, is very hard. If a successful identification is achieved, the current legal framework for seeking damages and other penalties is not particularly effective.

Sabotage

Sabotage involves the disconnection, unauthorised modification or damage to equipment, facilities or data. A certain degree of sabotage can be done without a physical presence. A hacker with malicious intent can disrupt the operation of critical items by, for example, corrupting password files, modifying parameters or injecting malicious code.

The most serious sabotage occurs when an individual obtains access to a computer room by, for example, pretending to be a maintenance engineer. If security is lax and the person is not accompanied and monitored, massive damage can be carried out in a very short time in such a way that it will not be discovered for several hours.

Any attack on a critical infrastructure should, by its very nature, be considered as an act of sabotage.

Anonymity

This has been discussed earlier. Other methods to ensure anonymity include the theft and/or cloning of cell-phones and the hijacking of a legitimate user's identity and password.

Data related offences

These can be divided in three main groups: interception and monitoring of data traffic, modification of data and data theft.

Interception of data

These offences involve the interception (tapping) of voice and fax messages, e-mail and data transfers.

Similarly, password sniffers are programs that monitor and record the names and passwords of network users as they log on. The security of the site is thus weakened as the recipient of this information can then impersonate the legitimate user and access restricted documents and perform transactions.

Monitoring of data traffic

There are many techniques that can be used to intercept data travelling between authorised origin and destination sources. These include:
- The theft of a physical medium in transit (for example backup tapes being taken to the off-site location where they are stored)
- Wiretapping – where an unauthorised entity monitors and records the data flowing between two points
- Intrusion – when access to the system or data flow circumvents a system's security features

There are many other forms of monitoring of data traffic that can include:
- Keystroke logging
- The scanning and filtering of e-mail traffic by organizations other than those of the sender and recipient (such as Internet Service Providers, governments and/or their intelligence services)
- The tracking of the websites visited by an individual, including pages consulted, how much time is spent on them, etc. This can be done by an employer as well as by the owner of a website interested in learning about the usage patterns of individuals.

Modification of data

The most common situation arises when a computer system is used to commit fraud by creating false transactions or modifying data to benefit one or more individuals.

Industrial espionage

It would seem that many people just love to spy... The emergence of a global network of networks, like the Internet, has created a totally new environment where professional hackers-for-money can search for, find and remove information about, product development, commercial strategies, staff salaries, and other confidential matters.

Professional hackers can do this leaving little or no evidence of theft and, as above, in the unlikely event of identifying the guilty party, legislation has not yet been written to cope with issues of electronic theft.

Software piracy and other copyright infringement

It is remarkably easy to make a copy of software and distribute it to others. This has been common since the early 1980s and the introduction of the personal computer, and continues to be practiced in many countries.

The pirating of high value software (computer aided design, digital photography workshops and toolboxes, financial accounting packages, etc) represents a substantial loss to the companies developing and marketing such applications.

Copied software works as well as the original and can be purchased for a fraction of the price. The chances of being found and prosecuted are relatively small.

Pirated software is sold in many countries and while the authorities have taken action against this, the business continues to flourish.

Tracking code

The World Wide Web Consortium has defined a standard for "cookies", a mechanism that allows the server to store information about a user on the user's own computer.

Cookies are simple text files stored on the end user's hard disk and they have many legitimate and beneficial uses, such as customising the content of a web page for an individual. A cookie tells the website that it's **you** who is looking at it.

Undeleted cookies build a complete history of where you have been on the web – and many of these cookies are placed by companies who advertise on the web, and keep enormous databases of who looks at what.

Browsers can also be exploited as a surveillance tool: your browser can tell others how you access the web, what software and hardware you are using, details of the link you have clicked on and possibly even your e-mail address.

In addition to browsers and cookies, there is extensive use of software such as "Web Bugs" (a one pixel by one pixel transparent graphic in GIF format) placed on a website or an e-mail. This is invisible to the user because it is transparent and very small (it can only be detected by looking at the source version of a web page).

Web-Bugs can be used to gather the following information:
- The IP address of the computer that "caught" the bug
- The URL of the page that the Web Bug is located on
- The time the Web Bug was viewed
- The type of browser that fetched the Web Bug image
- A previously set cookie value was caught

Proponents of privacy on the Internet object to the use of Web Bugs. On the other hand, these bugs can also be used to track copyright violations on the Web.

E-mail related offences

Mail Spamming

It is relatively easy to write software that automates the process of repeatedly sending e-mail to a large number of recipients, usually unsolicited commercial e-mail. It is also possible to use, without permission, other peoples' computers to send large amounts of mail to an individual.

Snooping of e-mail messages

An ordinary e-mail message is today's equivalent to a machine-readable postcard.

The machines that read them are either known to exist (Carnivore) or suspected (Echelon and similar in other parts of the world). At this time, the dividing line between the legality of a government owned machine and a privately owned one is unclear.

It does not require much knowledge to identify from the e-mail header the IP address from which it originated, and the route it took to reach the recipient.

Faked e-mail

The 'From" line in an e-mail message can be faked in several ways:
- Spoofing
- Remailing
- Relaying
- Stealing accounts
- Bogus accounts

Spoofing of e-mail messages consists of making a message appear to have come from somewhere or someone else. Spoofing is easy. The sender uses a software tool that is readily available on the Web to cut out the original IP address and replace it with someone else's address.

The good news is that spoofing is also relatively easy to deal with: the first server to receive the spoofed message records the real IP address of the sender, and this can be used to trace the original sender.

A *remailer* is a computer that strips the sender's IP address and then remails the message with the IP address of the remailer. The only way to find out who sent the message is to get access to the logs of the remailer – except that, designed to be anonymous, they don't log e-mail that has passed through that source. Anonymous remailers are used extensively by organised crime and terrorists as a means to hide in cyberspace.

Relaying consists of misusing someone else's e-mail server, something often done by spammers. A correctly configured e-mail server will not accept e-mail from IP addresses originating from outside its network. Unfortunately, not all e-mail servers are correctly configured to do so.

Stealing accounts requires the offender to gain access to someone else's e-mail account and password details, either by looking over someone's shoulder, or more technically, by sniffing a network to intercept such details.

Once someone has a legitimate user ID and password, the whole e-mail system is compromised and all tracking will lead to the more than likely innocent victim whose account has been hijacked.

Bogus e-mail accounts are opened from, for example, free e-mail services such as Hotmail by giving a false identity and address. As these accounts can be accessed from any computer with access to the World Wide Web, it is difficult to catch someone who has done this since the e-mail provider never knows who opened the false account.

Other activities of doubtful legality

There are numerous other activities that take place on the World Wide Web which do not appear to fall under the above categories

and about which1 the law is not always clear. Concerning what constitutes an offence or a crime and under what jurisdiction. The debate continues on the following activities:
- Distasteful and/or controversial content (hate, pornography, etc)
- Arms and drugs trading
- Trading in antiquities and stolen goods
- Money laundering (including off-shore unregulated gambling)
- Political propaganda
- Disinformation

There is no doubt that human ingenuity will continue to create new offences.

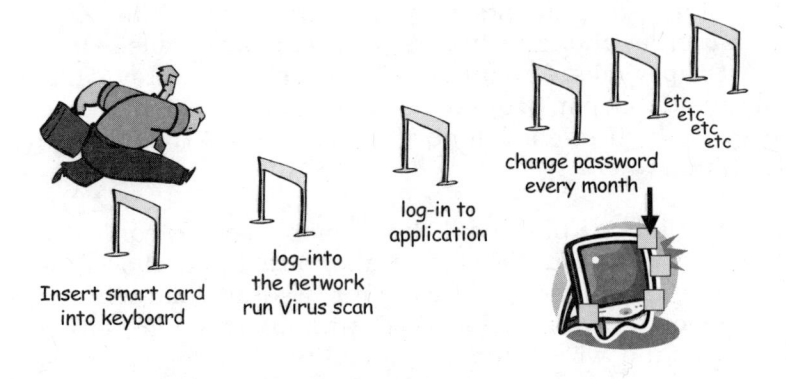

7. A SHORT HISTORY OF HACKING AND MALICIOUS CODE

The desire to make computer systems do things other than those for which they were designed has been around as long as computers. This section presents a short summary of this history. This section is based on a 1990 paper by Professor Dorothy Denning, entitled "Concerning hackers who break into computer systems", extended and updated for the preparation of this document.

1960s: The Dawn of Hacking

The first computer hackers emerge at MIT. They borrow their name from a term to describe members of a model train group at the school who "hack" the electric trains, tracks, and switches to make them perform faster and differently. A few of the members transfer their curiosity and rigging skills to the new mainframe computing systems being studied and developed on campus.

The malicious code of this time fell into two distinct categories: that designed to defraud the employer (back door, trap door, Trojan Horse) and that designed to blackmail or damage (Logic bomb).

1970s: Phone Phreaks and Cap'n Crunch

Phone hackers (phreaks or phreakers) break into regional and international phone networks to make free calls. One phreak, John Draper (aka Cap'n Crunch), learns that a toy whistle given away inside Cap'n Crunch cereal generates a 2600-hertz signal, the same high-pitched tone that accesses AT&T's long-distance switching system.

Draper builds a "blue box" that, when used in conjunction with the whistle and sounded into a phone receiver, allows phreaks to make free calls. Shortly thereafter, Esquire magazine publishes "Secrets of the Little Blue Box" with instructions for making a blue box, and wire fraud in the United States escalates. Among the perpetrators are two college kids (Steve Wozniak and Steve Jobs) later founders of Apple Computer, who launch a home industry making and selling blue boxes.

Malicious code in computing remained generally the same as in the 1960s.

1980s: Hacker Message Boards and Groups

Phone phreaks begin to move into the realm of computer hacking, and the first electronic bulletin board systems (BBSs) spring up.

The 8 bit personal computers had been around since the late 1970s and were popular with young technically minded people. electronic mail had also been around for some time and, in 1981, IBM introduced the 16 bit Personal Computer (PC) and allowed it to become an "open system," i.e. one that could be produced by other companies.

The precursor to Usenet newsgroups and e-mail, the boards--with names such as Sherwood Forest and Catch-22--become the venue of choice for phreaks and hackers to gossip, trade tips, and share stolen computer passwords and credit card numbers.

Hacking groups begin to form. Among the first are the "Legion of Doom" in the United States, and the "Chaos Computer Club" in Germany.

Worms are first used as a legitimate mechanism for performing tasks in a distributed environment. Network worms are considered promising for the performance of network management tasks in a series of experiments at the Xerox Palo Alto Research Center in 1982. The key problem is that of "worm management," controlling the number of copies executing at a single time. This would be taken advantage of later by authors of malicious worms.

1983: Kids' Games

The movie War Games introduces the public to hacking, and the legend of hackers as cyber-heroes (and anti-heroes) is born. The film's main character, played by Matthew Broderick, attempts to crack into a video game manufacturer's computer to play a game, but instead breaks into the military's nuclear combat simulator computer.

The computer (codenamed WOPR, a pun on the military's real system called BURGR) misinterprets the hacker's request to play Global Thermonuclear War as an actual enemy missile launch. The break-in throws the military into high alert, or Def Con 1 Defense Condition 1).

The same year, authorities arrest six teenagers known as the 414 gang (after the area code to which they are traced). During a nine-day spree, the gang breaks into some 60 computers, among them computers at the Los Alamos National Laboratory, which helps develop nuclear weapons.

This was a very interesting time. The term "computer virus" is formally defined by Fred Cohen in 1983, while performing academic experiments on a Digital Equipment Corporation VAX system.

Viruses are classified as being one of two types: research or "in the wild. " A research virus is one that has been written for research or study purposes and has received almost no distribution to the public. On the other hand, viruses which have been seen with any regularity are termed "in the wild."

The first computer viruses were developed in the early 1980s. The first viruses found in the wild were Apple II viruses, such as Elk Cloner, which was reported in 1981. Viruses have now been found on the following platforms: the Apple II, the Apple Mackintosh, the Atari, the Amiga and the IBM (and compatible) PCs.

1984: Hacker 'Zines

The hacker magazine *2600* begins regular publication, followed a year later by the online 'zine *Phrack*. The editor of 2600, "Emmanuel Goldstein" (whose real name is Eric Corley), takes his handle from the main character in George Orwell's 1984. Both publications provide tips for would-be hackers and phone phreaks, as well as commentary on the hacker issues of the day. Today, copies of *2600* are sold at most large retail bookstores.

1986: Use a Computer, Go to Jail

In the wake of an increasing number of break-ins to government and corporate computers, Congress passes the Computer Fraud and Abuse Act, which makes it a crime to break into computer systems. The law, however, does not cover juveniles.

The first IBM-PC virus – the Brain virus - appeared in 1986. Brain was a boot sector virus and remained resident. In 1987, Brain was followed by Alameda (Yale), Cascade, Jerusalem, Lehigh, and Miami (South African Friday the 13th).

These viruses expanded the target executables to include .COM and .EXE files. Cascade was encrypted to deter disassembly and detection.

1987: The Christmas Tree Exec "Worm"

Worms were first noticed as a potential computer security threat when the Christmas Tree Exec attacked IBM mainframes in December 1987. It brought down both the world-wide IBM network and BITNET. The Christmas Tree Exec wasn't a true worm. It was a trojan horse with a replicating mechanism. A user would receive an e-mail Christmas card that included executable (REXX) code. If executed the program claimed to draw a Xmas tree on the display. That much was true, but it also sent a copy to everyone on the user's address lists.

1988: The Morris Worm (also known as the Internet Worm)

Robert T. Morris, Jr., a graduate student at Cornell University and son of a chief scientist at a division of the National Security Agency, launches a self-replicating worm on the government's DARPAnet (the Defense Advanced Research Projects Agency network, the precursor to the Internet) to test its effect on UNIX systems.

The worm got out of hand and spread to some 6000 networked computers, clogging government and university systems. Morris was dismissed from Cornell, sentenced to three years' probation and fined $10,000.

The Father Christmas worm of December of 1988 was also a true worm. It was first released onto the worldwide DECnet Internet. This worm attacked VAX/VMS systems on SPAN and HEPNET. It utilized the DECnet protocols and a variety of system administration flaws to propagate. The worm exploited TASK0, which allows outsiders to perform tasks on the system. This worm added an additional feature: it reported successful system penetration to a specific site.

This worm made no attempt at secrecy; it was not encrypted and sent mail to every user on the system. About a month later another worm, apparently a variant of Father Christmas, was released on a private network. This variant searched for accounts with "industry standard" or easily guessed passwords.

1989: The Germans and the KGB

In the first cyber-espionage case to make international headlines, hackers in West Germany (loosely affiliated with the Chaos Computer Club) are arrested for breaking into U.S. government and corporate computers and selling operating-system source code to the Soviet KGB.

Three of them are turned in by two fellow hacker spies, and a fourth suspected hacker commits suicide when his possible role in the plan is publicized. Because the information stolen is not classified, the hackers are fined and sentenced to probation.

In a separate incident, a hacker is arrested who calls himself The Mentor. He publishes a now-famous treatise that comes to be known as the Hacker's Manifesto. The piece, a defense of hacker antics, begins, "My crime is that of curiosity ... I am a hacker, and this is my manifesto. You may stop this individual, but you can't stop us all."

With regard to malicious code, variable encryption also first appears in 1989 with the 1260 virus. Stealth viruses, which employ various techniques to avoid detection, also first appears in 1989, such as Zero Bug, Dark Avenger and Frodo (4096 or 4K).

1990: Operation Sundevil

After a prolonged sting investigation, Secret Service agents swoop down on hackers in 14 U.S. cities, conducting early-morning raids and arrests.

The arrests involve organizers and prominent members of BBSs and are aimed at cracking down on credit-card theft and telephone and wire fraud. The result is a breakdown in the hacking community, with members informing on each other in exchange for immunity.

In 1990, self-modifying viruses such as Whale are introduced. The year 1991 brought the GP1 virus, which is "network-sensitive" and attempts to steal Novell NetWare passwords. Since their inception, viruses have become increasingly complex.

1993: Why Buy a Car When You Can Hack One?

During radio station call-in contests, hacker-fugitive Kevin Poulsen and two friends rig the stations' phone systems to let only their calls through, and "win" two Porsches, vacation trips, and $20,000.

Poulsen, already wanted for breaking into phone- company systems, serves five years in prison for computer and wire fraud. (Since his release in 1996, he has worked as a freelance journalist covering computer crime.)

The first Def Con hacking conference takes place in Las Vegas. The conference is meant to be a one-time party to say good-bye to BBSs (now replaced by the Web), but the gathering is so popular it becomes an annual event.

1994: Hacking Tools R Us

The Internet begins to take off as a new browser, Netscape Navigator, makes information on the Web more accessible. Hackers take to the new venue quickly, moving all their how-to information and hacking programs from the old BBSs to new hacker Web sites.

As information and easy-to-use tools become available to anyone with Net access, the face of hacking begins to change.

1995: Catching Kevin Mitnick

Serial cyber-trespasser Kevin Mitnick is captured by federal agents and charged with stealing 20,000 credit card numbers. He's kept in prison for four years without a trial and becomes a cause célèbre in the hacking underground.

After pleading guilty to seven charges at his trial in March 1999, he's eventually sentenced to little more than the time he has already served while awaiting trial and fined just over 4,000 dollars. Not everyone is in agreement with his imprisonment.

Russian crackers siphon $10 million from Citibank and transfer the money to bank accounts around the world. Vladimir Levin, the 30-year-old ringleader, uses his work laptop after hours to transfer the funds to accounts in Finland and Israel. Levin stands trial in the United States and is sentenced to three years in prison. Authorities recover all but $400,000 of the stolen money.

1997: Hacking AOL

AOHell is released, a freeware application that allows a burgeoning community of unskilled hackers--or script kiddies--to wreak havoc on America Online. For days, hundreds of thousands of AOL users find their mailboxes flooded with multi-megabyte mail bombs and their chat rooms disrupted with spam messages.

1998: The Cult of Hacking and the Israeli Connection

The hacking group Cult of the Dead Cow releases its Trojan Horse program, Back Orifice - a powerful hacking tool - at Def Con. Once a hacker installs the Trojan horse on a machine running Windows 95 or Windows 98, the program allows unauthorized remote access of the machine.

During heightened tensions in the Persian Gulf, hackers touch off a string of break-ins to unclassified Pentagon computers and steal software programs. Then-U.S. Deputy Defense Secretary

John Hamre calls it "the most organized and systematic attack" on U.S. military systems to date.

An investigation points to two American teens. A 19-year-old Israeli hacker who calls himself The Analyzer (aka Ehud Tenebaum) is eventually identified as their ringleader and arrested. Today Tenebaum is chief technology officer of a computer consulting firm.

1999: Software Security Goes Mainstream. Who are the electrohippies?

In the wake of Microsoft's Windows 98 release, 1999 becomes a banner year for security (and hacking). Hundreds of advisories and patches are released in response to newfound (and widely publicized) bugs in Windows and other commercial software products. A host of security software vendors release anti-hacking products for use on home computers.

At the same time, computer systems are increasingly becoming homogeneous, and the exchange of executable programs through floppy disks is much less dominant than hitherto, with users being connected through networks and tighter control of software licensing and central software distribution. Viruses continue to appear.

Examples from the IBM-PC family of viruses indicate that the most commonly detected viruses vary according to continent. Stoned, Brain, Cascade, and members of the Jerusalem family, have spread widely and continue to appear. These are reasonably well dealt with by Anti-Virus software.

On March 26, 1999, a new type of infection emerged: An e-mail containing as an attachment an "infected" Microsoft Word document. This infection took advantage of a known design flaw in Microsoft Word and it required human action, i.e. the opening of the infected document for the virus to propagate. This became known as the Melissa (macro) Virus, and it spread itself to the first 50 addresses in the recipients' Microsoft Outlook directory.

Melissa takes four days to become prevalent and causes an estimated US $385 million worth of damage. David L. Smith, arrested after an investigation into the release of this virus, confessed to being its author and was released on bail of US $ 100,000 in December 1999. By August 2001, he was still free on bail and the date for sentencing remains undefined.

In early December 2001, the World Trade Organization's Seattle Conference is subject to disruptions, involving demonstrations, violent at times in an attempt to disrupt the conference. In addition to these physical interventions, one website urged WTO protesters to help tie up the WTO's Web servers.

The site, set up by a group calling themselves the Electrohippies, called it a virtual sit-in. By clicking on the sit-in link, a user's computer would be used to request information continually from WTO servers, tying up the user's Internet connection. This was essentially the use of hacker's denial-of-service techniques to perform an act of (in their words) civil disobedience in the shape of an electronic sit-in.

2000: Service is Denied, Love hurts and Hacktivism emerges

In February 2000 hackers launch one of the biggest distributed denial-of-service attacks to date against eBay, Yahoo, Amazon, and others causing major business disruption to the owners of these websites.

Whilst this was seen by most as an act of vandalism, there were a number of different views as to why these specific companies were targetted. One anarchist point of view is that they were attacked because the Internet has become the new tool for exploiting mankind and that the emergence of e-commerce is killing the hopes that others had for the Internet.

In May 2000 a new virus, called "I Love You", also affects thousands of corporate websites, and many companies have to shut down their e-mail systems in an effort to stop its spread. A leading vendor of Anti-Virus software, Symantec, states that in terms of spreadability, the "I Love You" virus outranked anything seen so far. Unlike Melissa, this virus has the ability to destroy data, in particular pictures and music files.

Onel de Guzman, a computer programming student in the Philippines was identified as the author of the virus and later arrested. Because of the lack of computer crime legislation in the Philippines, he was released shortly afterwards without charges. Although there is speculation that authorities in other countries would raise charges against de Guzman, this is not the case.

In the year 2000, Activists in Pakistan and the Middle East deface Web sites belonging to the Indian and Israeli governments to protest oppression in Kashmir and Palestine.

In October 2000, hackers break into Microsoft's corporate network and access source code for the latest versions of Windows and Office. This attack goes unnoticed for several weeks before Microsoft discovers it.

2001: Virus infections become a serious threat. Hacktivism comes of age.

In February 2001, a virus, encrypted and embedded in a photograph of Russian tennis player Anna Kournikova, spreads aggressively through e-mail – twice as fast as the "I Love You" virus. This virus uses a Visual Basic script to infect Windows based systems, and whenever the Microsoft Outlook e-mail program is used, it remails itself to the entire address book. This virus did not damage the systems it infected.

At the time, it was believed that the Kournikova virus had been manufactured using a "Virus creation kit" – a set of programs that let any on-line vandal with rudimentary computer skills to create malicious code. It was in fact produced by the 20-year-old Jan de Wit in the Netherlands who was sentenced to 150 hours of community service. He is appealing against this sentence.

In July 19, 2001, the Code Red self-replicating worm is released. This exploits a known vulnerability in Microsoft IIS servers, a product commonly used for websites. Code Red infiltrates

300,000 servers in only 14 hours, an unprecedented speed and slows the whole Internet.

The company Information Extraction and Transport, which conducts Internet epidemiology research for the Defense Advanced Research Projects Agency (DARPA), said about Code Red:

"Imagine a cold that kills. It spreads rapidly and indiscriminately through droplets in the air and you think you're absolutely healthy until you start to sneeze. Your only protection is complete, impossible, isolation.

Although the effects of Code Red did not last, some 6 million IIS servers worldwide had to be checked and upgraded to plug the security hole exploited by Code Red at an estimated cost of some 10 billion US dollars.

On 18 September 2001, a new infection emerges: the NIMDA worm. What was new about NIMDA was that
- It can spread through multiple mechanisms: via e-mail, by being connected through a common network, such as a Local Area Network and by browsing a compromised website.
- It is fully automated and does not require human intervention (such as opening an attachment) to spread itself.

NIMDA contains a sophisticated mechanism for collecting e-mail addresses from the infected computer but does not destroy data in the infected computer. It spreads more quickly than Code Red as it generates an avalanche of Internet traffic affecting both servers and clients. The sources of Code Red and NIMDA are still unknown.

There are serious concerns being expressed that Code Red and NIMDA were no more than test runs for new concepts in worm design. In such a scenario, we need to consider the possible (expected?) arrival of professionally designed, automatic attack worms that could not only paralyse the Internet but also carry a destructive payload that could affect a substantial part of the data accessible through the Internet.

The politics of hacking and cracking

Hacktivism represents a whole new level of activity on the World Wide Web. It is motivated by a political cause. This is electronic civil disobedience. If we had widespread use of computers and the Internet in the 60's, the anti war movement would have been carried out in cyberspace, not on America's college campuses.

There are many topics today – globalisation, human rights, the environment, and for each one of them there have been acts of electronic disobedience against it. Hacktivism is more oriented towards political causes throughout the world rather than protesting the alleged injustice of individuals and is truly global in character with examples such as The Anonymous Digital Coalition, consisting of The Hong Kong Blondes, X-ploit, The Cult of the Dead Cow, The Electric Disturbance Theatre, and many others. It is likely that the medium of the Internet will continue to be exploited for the purposes of civil disobedience and propaganda.

THE SOLUTION

So we now know how deep the problem is, and how vulnerable the information systems and networks on which we rely really are.

The question then is what are the possible solutions that can help us prevent breakdowns, and how speedily they can be actually put into place.

This is obviously a professional job. It requires detailed awareness of the dangers, and a willingness to draft and implement an information security strategy within a specific time frame.

It also requires the identification of the person who will be placed in charge of this effort and is responsible for its implementation, liable for any absence of due diligence or negligence or, in the most serious cases, for aiding and abetting cyber-crime or cyber-terrorism.

8. MANAGING INFORMATION SECURITY

Managing information security is more than a discipline: it is a way of life.

Its purpose is to achieve and maintain a state of equilibrium between four factors:

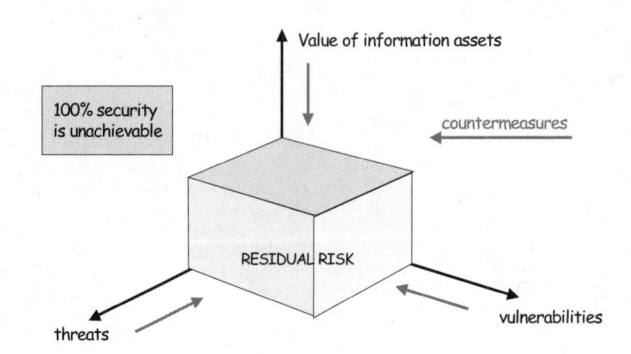

What are the **threats** to protect against and how likely are these?

These threats include all of the "bad guys" described above. Having identified them, it is necessary to understand what interest or grudges they may have in an organisation. This requires the assessment of the financial, social and operational impact of such a threat.

What are the **vulnerabilities** of the information infrastructure and operations of a particular organisation?

These vulnerabilities include technologies, software and operational practices, all of which are vulnerable to attack by an expert. Just as important is the degree to which best practices are applied, for example in configuration management and change control.

A less than robust response to an attack should also be considered vulnerability.

What is the **value** of the information assets to be protected?

This is a hard question to answer, as there are no agreed metrics for the value of information, information systems and, often, intellectual property. The methods to determine this value invariably include the cost of employee time when unable to perform their function. In the U.S.A., the figure of 1 dollar a minute is widely used.

How much **should be spent** on providing information security?

There is no right answer to this question. One of the many problems facing professionals is that budgets containing new expenditures to improve security are challenged by requesting a calculation of Return on Investment.

The response that "we spent half a million Euro last year and we believe that we have not been hacked" is unlikely to impress a Chief Financial Officer.

Ownership of information security processes

None of the guidelines and recommendations in this section will be of much use unless there is a clearly identified responsibility for security. Executives should not only assign overall responsibility to a single manager, typically the Chief Information Officer, although in a growing number of organizations, information security is managed separately from the ICT function with an overall Chief Security Officer.

In both cases, the person responsible for information security should be required to create and maintain a catalog of all known information systems and network vulnerabilities and certify in writing the security status of all the organization's systems. This is no different from requiring the Chief Information Officer to formally certify the organization's accounts.

Questions that executives should consider reviewing in their own organizations include:
- Who is responsible for the organization's overall information security at how is this responsibility dealt with at the organization's various locations?
- Who does the person responsible for the overall information security report to?

- Who reviews this person's performance and monitors her/his effectiveness?
- How is security managed with contractors, temporary personnel and outsource service providers?
- Who is responsible for dealing with a security incident?
- Who is responsible for conducting information security tests and audits?
- What is the organization's policy with regards to compliance with security policies and practices?

When there are unambiguous answers to all these questions, the executive would have acted with due diligence and established an organizational framework that will support the practice of information security throughout the organization.

The components of managing information security

Information Security management can be grouped into three main activities:
- Risk assessment, policy definition, planning and implementation
- Operation, audit, testing and certification
- Responding to an event, post-mortem and digital forensics

The reader is referred to ISO 17799, an international standard on the Management of Information Security as a comprehensive guide to implementation. The next section presents an outline of what the standard contains and what it means in practice.

In addition there are several technical standards such as X.509, defining digital certificates, and the X.800 series of recommendations of the ITU, the International Telecommunications Union, as well as a number of vendor developed proposed and de-facto standards, such as the proposed standard WS-Security jointly developed by IBM and Microsoft, recently joined by Verisign.

While standards and legislation are both important components and a strong base on which to build, these are not enough by themselves to provide security. An outline of the main activities in the management of information security is given in the sections that follow.

9. ISO CODE OF PRACTICE FOR INFORMATION SECURITY

The Geneva based International Standards Organization (ISO) published this document in 1999. Its precursor was the British Standard BS 7799 (Part I), the British Standards Institute Code of Practice for Information Security Management, first issued in 1995 subsequently adopted in slightly modified form by a number of other countries.

ISO 17799 identifies and describes ten guiding principles as the basis of a system for the management of Information Security. A summary of each of these principles is presented in this Chapter.

Although described as a standard, ISO 17799 is not prescriptive, for example:
- It does not state "you must have a firewall", instead it says "precautions are required to prevent and detect the introduction of malicious software"
- It does not say that "**your** system must be the same as **my** system", instead it says that "It is essential that an organization identifies **its** security requirements"

Guiding Principle No.1. Security policy

Purpose: to provide management direction and support for information security

The standard recommends the following framework
- Establishment of a top-level management security forum
- Provision of individual security awareness training
- Risk management as a management approach
- Compliance with the appropriate legislation (e.g. Data Protection Act)

A policy document would normally contain sections on:
- The need for an organization to have a contingency plan

- The need for effective data back-up
- The avoidance of malicious software
- Procedures for controlling access to systems and data
- Procedures for the reporting of security incidents
- Procedures for non-compliance with the policy, malicious activity, inappropriate use, etc

Guiding Principle No. 2. Security organization

Purpose: to manage information security within the organization with particular emphasis on:
1. maintaining the security of organizational information processing facilities and of assets accessed by third parties
2. maintaining the security of information when the responsibility for information processing and service delivery has been outsourced to another organization.

Such a security organization needs to make provision for, at a very minimum:
- Establishment of an internal forum for information security
- Arrangements for the coordination of information security
- Allocation of information security responsibilities to nominated functions/ individuals
- Identification of the risks associated with third party access to data and information
- Ensuring that security requirements are specified in contracts with third parties
- Security requirements in outsourcing contracts

Guiding Principle No. 3. Asset classification and control

Purpose: to identify the scope of information security management and ensure that information assets are given an appropriate level of protection.

An organization implementing ISO 17799 must determine which of its information assets may materially impact the operation and delivery of the organization's activities or business if they were to be unavailable or degraded.

This in turn, requires an analysis of the probability (risk assessment) that a given threat will exploit a specific weakness to cause loss or damage to an asset or group of assets. Risk is defined by the combination of value, vulnerability and threat.

All assets relevant to the scope of the Information Security Management System must be identified and have a nominated "owner" or custodian.

Guiding Principle No. 4. Personnel security

Purpose: to reduce the risks of human error, theft, fraud or misuse of facilities, in particular,
1. by ensuring that all end-users are aware of information security threats and concerns and that they can support the organization's security policies in the course of their normal work
2. by working to minimise the damage caused by security incidents and malfunctions as well as to learn from such incidents

Typically, the tasks to be undertaken to meet this requirement are:
- The inclusion of security considerations and responsibilities in job descriptions and staff contracts
- End-user training
- Response methodologies and practices in the event of malfunctions and security incidents

Guiding Principle No. 5. Physical and environmental security

Purpose: to prevent unauthorised access, damage and interference to business premises and information and, as a result:
1. prevent loss, damage or compromise of assets and/or an interruption to business activities

2. prevent the theft of information and/or information processing facilities

Normal practices in the implementation of environmental security include:
- Definition and implementation of a security perimeter
- Physical access controls (e.g. smart cards, keypad and secret codes and their associated monitoring)
- Definition of secure working areas and associated practices
- Ensuring the continuity and security of power supplies
- Practices for the disposal of equipment (which may contain licensed software and data falling under the scope of the security policy)

Guiding Principle No. 6. Communications and operations management

Purpose: to ensure the correct and secure operation of information processing facilities to:
1. Minimise the risk of systems failures
2. Protect the integrity of software and information
3. Maintain the integrity and availability of information processing and communications facilities
4. Ensure the safeguarding of information in networks
5. Ensure the protection of the supporting infrastructure
6. Prevent damage to assets and interruptions to business activities
7. Present the loss, modification or misuse of information exchanges between organizations

The minimum components of such practices are:
- Fully documented operational procedures (typically including Availability and Performance Management, Incident and Problem Management, Change Control and Configuration Management among others)
- Clear assignments of responsibilities to individuals
- Protection against malicious software
- Housekeeping (for example, registering and maintaining the records of users, inventories, resource usage)

- Network management
- Media handling and its security
- Exchanges of information and software with other parties

Best practices in the above are extensively documented.

Guiding Principle No. 7. Access control

Purpose: to control access to information to:
1. Prevent unauthorised access to information systems
2. Prevent unauthorised computer access
3. Ensure the protection of networked services
4. Detect unauthorised activities
5. Ensure information security when using mobile computing and teleworking facilities

Even though individual users may have legitimate access to an organization's systems, data and information, their rights may not include universal access to all information assets.

Therefore, an organization needs to define who has the rights to access what and when.

The usual activities associated with access control include:
- Definition of the access control requirements (focus on confidentiality)
- Managing the access rights of individual users
- Defining the responsibilities of individual users
- Defining the appropriate mechanisms for access to a) the network, b) applications, c) operating systems
- Policies and practices for monitoring system access and use
- Policies and practices for granting remote access from teleworking staff, from mobile devices, etc

These issues require particular attention when these activities are outsourced and it is strongly recommended that the right to audit the outsourcer should be part of all such contracts.

Guiding Principle No. 8. Systems development and maintenance

Purpose: To ensure that security is built into information systems to:
1. Prevent loss, modification or misuse of user data in applications systems
2. Protect the confidentiality and integrity of information
3. Ensure information systems and support activities are conducted in a secure manner
4. Maintain the security of application system software and data throughout the lifecycle of such systems

This would normally require:
- Definition of the security requirements of systems and computer applications
- Definition of the role of cryptographic controls
- Ensuring the security of system files
- Ensuring the security of development and support processes

As in the case of 7 above, applications development is an activity which is increasingly being outsourced, and the same recommendation applies: that the right to audit the outsourcer should be part of all such contracts.

Guiding Principle No. 9. Business Continuity Management

Purpose: to counteract interruptions of business activities and protect critical business processes from the effects of major failures or disasters.

It is important to distinguish three distinct activities relating to this:
- Disaster Recovery: this is the responsibility of the parties providing communications and operations management, i.e. an essentially technical process that relies on the use of other, often distant, facilities with an adequate replica of the infrastructure.

- Business Continuity: the next level up from Disaster Recovery, where clearly defined and essential activities can continue to be carried out from another location. This is the responsibility of senior management and involves a number of staff who must be contactable and ready to assume these responsibilities as and when required.
- Crisis Management: another senior management responsibility, which involves communicating with all stakeholders and other interested parties once a disaster has been invoked and the business continuity arrangements put in place.

Guiding Principle No. 10. Compliance

Purpose: to avoid breaches of any civil or criminal law or of statutory, regulatory or contractual obligations, and to comply with organizational security policies and maximise the effectiveness of system audit processes.

This requires a thorough knowledge of the legislative framework in which the organization operates, as well as the review of the security policy from this perspective.

System audit becomes an essential part of the compliance process.

10. INFORMATION SECURITY IN THE CORPORATE ENVIRONMENT

The material in this section is divided in three parts (physical, logical and people security) and presented, from a managerial perspective in non-technical language.

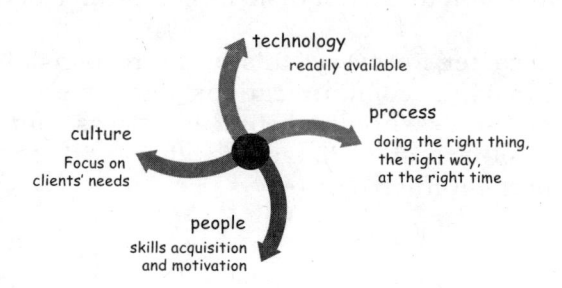

technology
readily available

process
doing the right thing,
the right way,
at the right time

culture
Focus on
clients' needs

people
skills acquisition
and motivation

General considerations

The implementation, operation and management of information security is more than a discipline. It is a way of life and relies on four components, all of which equally important and indispensable.

Processes are fundamentally important to all systematic and/or continuous operations. Standards such as those set by ISO are of great value. Processes must be systematically applied and reviewed in the light of experience to remove as many systematic errors and flaws as possible.

People (staff, contractors, consultants) are vital to all operations and services. They need to be present in adequate numbers and with appropriate skills, experience and motivation.

Technology is readily available. However, products are not perfect, and also have relatively short life cycles. The market is very competitive and a high percentage of vendors come and go – they are either absorbed by a bigger company or simply go out of business. All of this makes Technology Assessment more important than ever before.

Culture defines the work environment and in order to succeed, it must be shared across the organization. Executives have a major role to play in establishing and maintaining an appropriate culture.

Examples of cultures that have traditionally been successful in managing information security can be found in two main areas of activity:
- Intelligence, Defense and Police
- Banking, Foreign Exchange, Stock Markets and Insurance

The cultural aspects considered to be critical for the successful management of information security include:
- Full support and commitment to security from the very top management
- Strong organizational discipline

- Clearly documented and communicated policies
- Clearly documented processes supported by audits
- Systematic compliance monitoring
- Consistent actions to deal with non-compliance
- Regular tests, audits and reviews

Organizations that have implemented ISO standards are well placed to expand the culture this standard entails.

Physical security

Like the basic security measures taken in the home, physical security is a prerequisite. It serves to create an environment and visible culture of controlled access and preparedness for disruption and damage to equipment.

Best practices require the definition of, among others:
- Those individuals who may enter a computer room or data centre, and whether they can do so alone or accompanied at all times
- Those individuals who may physically access specific pieces of equipment, and under what circumstances
- The conditions under which other parties such as contractors, consultants, temporary staff, cleaners, etc may enter the facilities
- The conditions and practices for the disposal of equipment no longer required
- The conditions for transporting and storing physical media such as magnetic tapes containing data

as well as the necessary provision of:
- suitably selected, implemented, managed and monitored access control devices
- access control and/or identity cards or devices
- secure doors and other access points (e.g. for deliveries and removals)
- flooding, fire and smoke detectors, lighting and closed circuit television

- secured power supplies and appropriate backup (batteries and generators)
- suitable locked cabinets, cable trays and other similar engineering practices

These matters take on particular significance whenever the provision of computer room or data center services has been outsourced, in which case the right to audit the service provider becomes an important consideration.

Logical security

As stated earlier, information security does not require the attacker to have physical contact with the victim. Logical security is achieved when several complementary mechanisms are used together in an effective manner.

Logical security complements physical arrangements by providing procedures, tools and software to:
- structure how data and information are accessed and by whom
- create secure copies of all software and data to support disaster recovery create appropriate audit logs
- implement appropriate encryption mechanisms
- detect attempts to breach security or actual events
- detect malicious software within the systems, in electronic mail and in media

The following figure presents these major components of logical security.

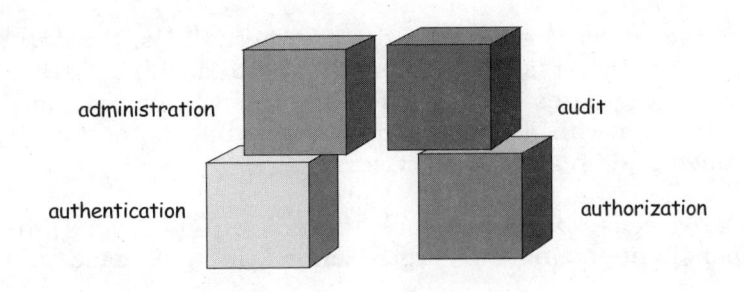

administration   audit

authentication   authorization

Authentication is the first component:

Who are you? Now prove it.

In order to prove to a computer system who you are, there are three possible approaches:

1. Tell the system something <u>you know</u>: a name and a password.

Passwords are simple to implement but they have shortcomings:

They can be disclosed to a third party, for example by a disgruntled or ex-employee. They can be subject to complex rules: minimum number of characters, not easy to guess terms or dates, mix of letters and numbers, changed every month, etc. In these cases there is a strong temptation to write passwords down, which defeats the object if someone else finds them

2. Provide the system something <u>you have</u>: an identity card or a token.

Security can be increased by requiring, in addition to the password, some kind of physical device such as an electronic identity card or token.

3. Give the system something <u>you are</u>

Personal features such as a retinal scan or voice pattern, called "biometrics," can be used in truly high security environments. The technologies are complex and expensive. Despite this, their use is increasing.

Once the system knows who the user actually is, the natural next question is "what is this person allowed to do": the **Authorisation** process regulates access to resources, for example what transactions can be performed and what data can be seen, modified and created by the user.

Such *access privileges* are based on a user's role and responsibilities in the organization. In the case of service providers such as libraries, e-commerce companies, etc. such privileges are determined by criteria such as contracts, subscriptions, credit worthiness, credit history, etc.

Administration is the process of maintaining users' profiles as well as managing the security definitions of a particular resource. This includes such activities as removing the access privileges of an employee who is leaving the company, changing the profiles and the list of systems a specific user is allowed to access following a promotion or transfer, etc.

Particular care has to be taken to plan the strategy to be followed in the case of a replacement of the Administrator himself.

Audit is the confirmation that these security measures are reasonable and in working order. There is no way to know if a user is exceeding authorization without such audits. There is also no way to show where security measures should be strengthened without first knowing where they are weak. Audit is a vital complement to all security measures.

None of the measures above will be effective without a number of people-oriented features:
- Executive support for information security policies, measures and processes must be fully committed *before* a security incident takes place.
- Staff needs to be aware of the threats related to information security and their importance of information security to their organization
- Staff needs to be organised, skilled and trained for dealing with information security incidents
- All such training on information security must be consistent with the needs of the organization
- Due consideration must also be given to other people with access to the organization's information assets such as maintenance personnel, consultants, contractors, temporary staff, cleaners, and others.

The delicate issues of pre-recruitment security clearances, the right to privacy in the workplace, the conduct of investigations, etc., are major topics in their own right.

The list below highlights those activities, which the executive must control in order to ensure the success of information security management.

Understanding the use of information systems and technology

Such an understanding should not be from a technical perspective (who uses what software) or what kind of equipment staff have on
their desk.

What is meant here includes a good knowledge of
- what would be the impact of a major security incident on the image and reputation of the organization, on its financial and operational performance, etc?
- how critical to the organization and the constituencies it supports are the use of computer systems and facilities such as the World Wide Web, Internet mail, multimedia facilities, etc?
- how well does the organization comply with appropriate legislation (for example data protection)?
- what are the organization's legal liabilities associated with such matters?

The following are the prerequisites for the development of effective information security policies:

Conducting a risk assessment, in particular looking for vulnerabilities

This is a process that should be carried out on a regular basis to look for glaring problems such as poor password practices, missing updates and patches in infrastructure facilities, unauthorised dial-up modems and other "back doors" to the corporate network

Developing and implementing proper policies

This action is the first requirement of ISO 17799. Documented policies are essential if information security is to be successful. It is the only effective way to deal with the excuse, "I did not know".

Such policies must be based on business needs and relate to business risk and must be understood and supported by the executive, whose commitment to security is essential. This will only occur when the executive recognises that information security is not just a "technical matter" that is fixed by installing a firewall.

It is usual practice that staff and other parties should sign an acknowledgement of receipt of such policies and a commitment to comply with them, including the acceptance of the measures the organization may take in the event of non-compliance.

Like any other process oriented documentation there is a risk that the creation, maintenance and dissemination of such policies may create its own bureaucracy. Good judgment is necessary to keep things in proportion. The effort required to create and maintain workable policies should not be underestimated.

Many templates for such policies are available and can be useful to establish such policies. However, the value of the policies will be determined by how successfully they are communicated and applied.

A document based on a template and kept in a bookshelf ("Shelfware") may satisfy an inexperienced auditor that one has a security policy, but it has no business value.

The publication of a security policy must be supported by a security awareness campaign and the briefing of all staff and other interested parties. This is a particularly important step in the recruitment of new staff.

Define accountability for managing information security

The story of the job that needed to be done and the four people who were there at the time: Messrs. Anybody, Somebody, Everybody and Nobody is worth repeating:

> **Everybody thought that Somebody would do the job.
> In fact, Anybody could have done it.
> In the end Nobody did it.**

It would be disastrous if information security were to be managed in this way and avoidance of such a situation requires recognition that information security is not just an "IT problem" and that executives do not abdicate their responsibilities in this area.

Executives must define the business need and the value of the assets to be protected, make resources available to deploy the necessary security, test it and manage it, and remain its main client.

The CIO or other senior IT professional must play the roles of (a) champion of the information security measures and (b) chief coordinator for the organization.

The CIO must be accountable for the way in which all technical aspects are implemented and operated including technical choices, how and where security is sourced, what resources are assigned to it and how well it performs.

Other responsibilities of the CIO are arranging for network and other tests to identify security weaknesses and vulnerabilities, develop processes to improve the detection of malicious code and work to minimise false alarms.

It is also essential that the security organization should implement measures to make sure that the information resources of the organization have not been the subject of external or internal attacks.

Implementing appropriate security tools and procedures

The technical implementation of security will require the selection and procurement of a variety of products. These must have a demonstrable track record of effectiveness.

However, these products in and of themselves have limited value if they are not properly installed and configured. It is common practice for vendors to deliver these products in a standard configuration referred to as "Out of the Box" or "Shrink-wrapped", which include, amongst other features, an initial User ID and password for the security administrator, which is well known, particularly to hackers. These default values MUST be changed to approved criteria before these products are put into service.

Similarly, the CIO will be responsible for the development, introduction and management of processes to support the administration and monitoring of compliance with the security policy. These processes would normally include the critical task of monitoring incidents, events and trends, as well as following industry's alerts and notifications.

Best practices for such processes are based on using a central administration and distribution facility to ensure that all end-users have the latest updates of virus protection software and that they are immediately notified of infections.

Allowing vendors and maintenance organizations on-line access to support 24/7

High availability operations (99.95% and above) rely strongly on the technical support of vendors. To maintain these high levels of availability the former practice of a four-hour guaranteed response time will simply not do.

Vendors now rely on diagnostic features built into their equipment and software to provide real time information to their technical support organization, which typically operates from multiple locations, 24 hours a day 7 days a week, by direct on-line communications. This implies an exchange of data between your facility and that of the technical support organization of the vendor.

This is a back door into your organization and the security aspects of such access must be clearly specified in the contracts with the vendor and subject to audit by your chosen auditors.

11. GUIDELINES FOR SAFE COMPUTING

The previous pages describe a worrying scenario. In such circumstances, what should one do, at home, on the move and even at work to be confident that one's personal information is not stolen and misused, that one's data is not compromised or corrupted and that one can use the resources of the Internet with reasonable confidence?

The answers can be found in the following pages, which explore:
- Privacy and the Internet
- Tools and measures to protect one's systems and data from the offences most often found on the World Wide Web
- Good safe computing practices

Privacy and the Internet

It is clear that you would normally not give out personal information on the phone, through the mail or over the Internet unless you've initiated the contact, or know with whom you are dealing.

Life on the Internet however is, different. There are many parties who are interested in who you are and what you do on the Web, all with different intentions. It is because of this that initiatives such as the Electronic Privacy Information Center (EPIC) and the World Wide Web Consortium (W3C) Platform for Privacy Preferences (P3P) were launched.

Among the many examples of potential intrusions on your personal privacy include:

Details of your hardware and software configuration, the browser you use, your assigned IP (Internet Protocol) address are readily available to the websites you visit. The IP address is usually sufficient to give an indication of your physical location.

Your IP address – which is included in every e-mail you send, can be used to reveal at least some information about your geographical location, and this may be useful when trying to trace a suspect message received.

The owner of a Website will want to know, for example, when you access the Website, what pages and documents you look at, whether you download items or not, whether you look at (click) advertisements, etc. To do this, they place cookies on your computer, and employ spy-ware and other devices to track such use.

The owner of a website who specialises in advertising, wants to know your e-mail address and so does a spammer. Many websites require individuals to register in order to provide access, usually free of charge to their site's content. Such registration requires details of name, address, and sometimes other personal information such as age and marital status and e-mail address.

The issue of potential invasion of privacy is raised when such information willingly provided by the visitor to the Website is subsequently matched against other commercially available sources of information (e.g. demographic to build a more detailed profile of individuals which is stored in electronic databases and which may be made available to other parties.)

The owner of a website dealing with electronic commerce needs to know your name, address, e-mail address, credit card number and period of validity and other related information.

There are other people whose interest may be somewhat less benign. Generally known under the name of "Pretexters" they may pose as representatives of survey firms, banks, Internet service providers and even government agencies to get you to reveal your

Social Security number or equivalent, mother's maiden name, financial account numbers and other identifying information.

Legitimate organizations with which you do business have the information they need and will not ask you for it.

It is interesting to note that hardly any websites provide their visitors with the ability to validate what personal information is held in the databases. In Europe this is in fact against the relevant Data Protection legislation, which allows for (at least limited) access to such information (e.g. the European Union's Data Protection Directive).

e-Mail related privacy issues

Who is reading your e-Mail?

The section on Information Security Players has described some of the tools that can be used to monitor the contents of e-mail messages (such as Carnivore and Echelon). Similar systems may be used by an employer to monitor the content of messages for abusive or improper language, personal rather than business use, etc.

Not all employers have clearly articulated policies about their rights and yours, and without such policies, many problems can arise, largely influenced by the national legislation concerning the rights of individuals. Such matters can become quite complex when, in the case of a telecommuter, the employer's e-mail system is used by a family member for personal matters.

Is someone forwarding your e-mails without your knowledge?

This is perhaps the most common source of trouble – and there have been many articles in the press – when an e-mail between two parties, intended to be a private exchange and essentially a confidential matter, is subsequently distributed by the recipient to third parties without the knowledge or consent of the sender.

Is someone sending e-mail on your behalf ?

The first indication you may have that someone is spoofing your mail or has stolen your account may be when you get into very serious trouble. If innocent, your only recourse is to ask for a full investigation, which may or may not be conclusive.

Are you receiving fake e-mail?

As above, you may not know unless there is something suspicious about the content or it turns out to contain malicious software. Again, should this happen, it is advisable to arrange for an investigation.

Tools and measures

A word of caution: the tools and technologies described in this section are, at best, not perfect. However good they are, it is imperative that they should be
- installed correctly
- regularly maintained
- configured to operate at their maximum performance.

Protecting against malicious code

The best form of protection against malicious code is the use of trusted quality Anti-Virus software. Such software is available commercially from a number of vendors as well as in the form of Freeware or Shareware. In general terms, even the most expensive commercial anti-virus software represents a fraction of the value of your computer, all of its software and, in particular, your data.

The practice of implementing a personal Firewall is also spreading and it is worth considering if you access the Internet through a dial-up connection. For any form of permanent connection, the use of a personal firewall is strongly recommended.

A personal firewall consists of software that protects a single Internet-connected computer from intruders. This protection is especially useful for individuals with "always-on" connections such as DSL or cable modem.

As in the case of anti-virus software, personal firewalls are available from several vendors and some of them can be downloaded from the Internet free-of-charge.

Software is not static, and both anti-virus products and personal firewalls are frequently revised and improved by their vendors. These improvements come in three distinct shapes:

Patch (sometimes called a "fix")

A quick-repair job for a piece of programming. Problems (bugs) are invariably found. A *patch* is the immediate solution that is provided to users; it can be usually downloaded from the software maker's website. The patch is not necessarily the best solution for the problem and the product developers often find a better solution later

New Release

A full edition of a software package that incorporates all patches and repairs, to a higher standard of resolution and, sometimes includes additional functionality.

Upgrade

A full edition of a software package that brings substantial new features to previous releases.

Whilst patches are usually free of charge to licensed users, new releases and upgrades must be purchased. Owners of previous versions of the software usually, but not always, can upgrade at a reduced cost.

The use of original, fully licensed software is essential in order to obtain such updates as well as technical support from their suppliers.

Protecting your privacy

Configure your personal computer features to avoid disclosure

You must configure your web browser to ensure that information you do not wish to share is not inadvertently made public: In your browser's configuration tool (which may be referred to as Options, Setup or Preferences, depending on which browser you use, you have the choice of using a pseudonym instead of your real name and of not entering an e-mail address or other personally identifiable information.

It is also a good practice to look at other "Internet-defaults" in your computer for example in Windows the "Internet Control Panel" and with an Apple "Configuration Manager" and "Internet Config". These can be made equally anonymous if they contain any fields for personal information.

In a domestic environment where a computer is shared by several people, it is important to set out clear rules so that everyone knows NOT to reveal personal information other than on an approved, website-by-website basis.

Employers' policies concerning monitoring

What you do in your home, through your personal access to the Internet and the Internet Service Provider of your choice, is usually your own business, unless your employer has advised you otherwise. Using your employer's corporate network from your home, or surfing the Web, downloading software and doing your personal e-mail, may be in conflict with the employer's security policies and practices. These policies should normally be clearly disclosed to all staff.

Privacy at work is a major topic in its own right, for which there are no fixed rules. Legislation on this matter is either incomplete or ambiguous with the exception of criminal or civil investigations when there is "sufficient cause". Otherwise, it is a matter for very clear communications between management and employees. It's wise to assume that there is NO privacy at work, and that this applies no only to computer systems, e-mail, etc., but also to the use of telephones and fax machines.

Cookie manager

Whilst cookies are well-defined standard features of the Internet, and when legitimately used, quite convenient. They can be abused. An example is the disclosure of information about your browsing habits to other interested parties, such as advertisers.

Moreover, cookie files in your computer constitute a record of your usage of the Internet that you may wish to, at the very least, have some control over. The mechanism to do this is cookie management software.

The latest versions of browsers (for example Internet Explorer v.6) include a cookie manager, which allows you to decide which cookies you wish to accept, view the cookies on your hard disk and to delete those you wish to remove. There are many other cookie managers that can be downloaded from the Internet, either free or requiring a modest registration fee.

User IDs and Passwords and/or physical devices

It is always a good idea to protect your computer, particularly notebooks and other small devices to prevent access by others.

Such protection can take many forms ranging from a well designed User ID and password to the use of physical devices such as Smart Cards or small pieces of hardware (commonly referred to as "dongles") that need to be physically plugged in, usually in a parallel port.

A good password needs to meet two requirements: it should not require you to write it down and it should not be easily guessed (first name, date or birth, name of a child) or broken (such as with a dictionary attack tool).

Generally accepted criteria are that a password should be at least six characters long and contain both characters and numbers.

Some systems are case sensitive and will also differentiate between upper-case and lower-case letters. Regrettably, these criteria can be incompatible with the human memory and our need to write such passwords down to be able to remember them when needed.

Memorising multiple passwords becomes an even bigger headache unless you create a personal mnemonic system as an aid.

It is also good practice to password protect specific documents that you do not wish others to share.

Encryption and other privacy tools

Hiding your text or files with a password is a good practice but not necessarily a highly secure one. There are two important kinds of encryption:

Digital Signatures, allow you to verify that a message was written by the person it claims to be from and that it has not been modified during transmission.

Digital signatures use a pair of keys, a public one which you provide to everyone (for example by posting it on your personal web page) and a private or secret key, known only to one individual and kept in this person's personal computer in encrypted form requiring a "pass-phrase" to activate it.

Anyone can send a private message encrypted with the public key. Only the genuine recipient of this message can read it with the private key. To send a personal digital signature to someone else, one must use the private key. The recipient can confirm that it came from this individual by testing it with the public key.

It is essential that whatever software is used to create digital signatures be trusted to use secure techniques and be a robust well-supported and studied design. A product such as Pretty Good Privacy (PGP) is widely acknowledged to meet these requirements and is available free of charge for non-commercial use.

Tools are available to create a secure space on a hard disk to store sensitive information, often requiring a private key to provide access to it.

A Digital Certificate is an electronic file that uniquely links a person to a public key and is a device extensively used in electronic commerce. The subject of Public Key Infrastructure (PKI), its operation and trustworthiness is beyond the scope of this publication.

Cryptography, is the second mechanism for ensuring privacy since the invention of writing and has been in used in many different forms. Cryptography is usually reserved for the most highly confidential messages and has a counterpart in Cryptanalysis, the process of braking ciphers – something that is not always possible (at present).

Sophisticated encryption devices and software are currently classified as weapons by several countries and require an export license, which, in the U.S.A. is issued by the State Department – an authorization that appears difficult to obtain. In reality, exporting software either on a floppy disk or by a file transfer is not difficult and is used to circumvent the authorization process.

Encryption is used to protect information about credit card details in transmission to the website. However it does not ensure that the website stores the information securely. Many e-commerce and other websites have been broken into by crackers, and as a result thousands of credit card details have been stolen, as was the case at the 2001 meeting of the World Economic Forum at Davos, Switzerland.

Credit card number details should NEVER be disclosed without making sure first that the connection is in fact encrypted – this is usually indicated by an icon such as a closed lock or padlock or an unbroken key as well as by a web address (URL which begins with http**s**//: -- if the web address does not have this "**s**" at the end of the "http" is not a secure site.

Protecting your use of e-mail

E-mail messages to unknown parties such as newsgroups, chat rooms and other public spaces need not be in your real name. For these situations, it is convenient to have one or more alternate accounts, often, but not necessarily, using a pseudonym. Addresses that are widely posted become targets for on-line junk mailers, known as spammers. If you become their target, simply ditch the account and open a new one from one of the many free offerings available.

Understanding headers

e-Mail headers can tell you many things: the route a message took to get to your e-mail account, where the message originated, what e-mail program was used to send it, and more. But how do you know what the header contains?

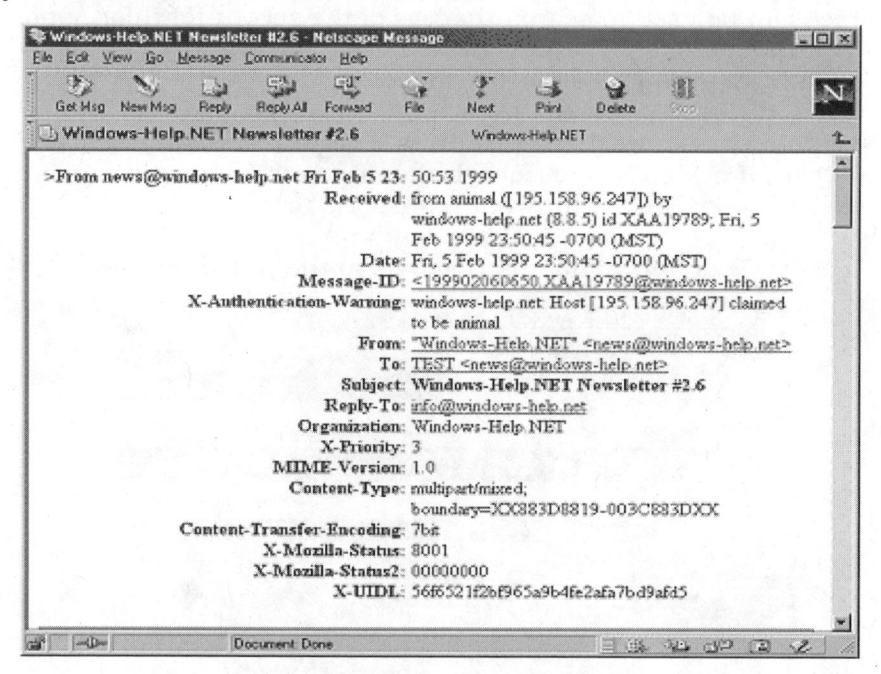

Most e-mail programs give you an option to "Show all headers", and in Microsoft's Outlook Express it's just a matter of pressing **Ctrl+F3** while selecting a message. This will open a separate window, where you can view all the header information. In Netscape Messenger, you can select the **View > Headers**, and make a selection from **Brief, Normal** or **All**. There are a wide variety of e-mail headers and some programs use/display different headers than others. The principles are the same.

The example shown above has a header which indicates first which Account received the message, and at which Date and Time.

The next header is the Received: header, which is the last *host* passed by the message before being placed in your mailbox. Here the message was from a machine with the name animal, with the I.P. address 195.158.96.247. It was received by windows-help.net, on Friday 5 February 1999, at 23:50:45 (MST), which is 7 hours (0700) behind Greenwich Mean Time.

Message-ID: Each message is given a unique ID by the server, which can be used to search the logs of the server, for information about the message. The next headers (From:, To:, Subject, Reply-To: and Organization) are self evident.

Now that you know the I.P. address where the e-mail originated, you can, if in doubt, crosscheck the originator's domain name to see if it is consistent with what it purports to be.

An example of how to do this is shown in the picture below.

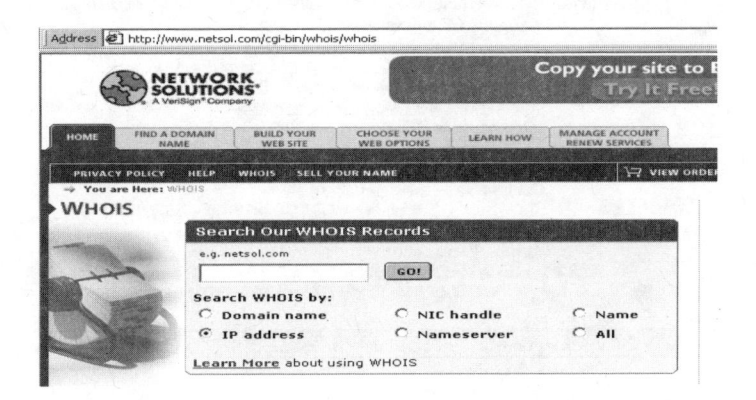

At this point, you should be aware of the bad news:

A good hacker or spammer will not find it difficult to forge the message headers by tampering with the SMTP server (**S**imple **M**ail **T**ransport **P**rotocol).

Good Safe Computing Practices

Ensure that you have all the material necessary to rebuild your software and:
- Consider not being "permanently connected" as you are with DSL and cable modems. Such connections use a static IP address that makes them especially vulnerable to potential hackers.
- Ensure your Internet browser is sufficiently recent to incorporate security features and make certain these are correctly configured in your computer (examples: Internet Explorer later than version 5.5 and Netscape Navigator later than version 6.0).
- Keep copies of all original and licensed software, together with appropriate ID codes and documentation needed to obtain updates and technical support.
- Ensure that your freeware (software downloaded free of charge from the Internet) is from a reputable and recommended source and that your shareware (software downloaded free of charge from the Internet but for which a modest registration or usage fee is required) meets the same criteria as freeware AND is registered with the provider.
- Look for and install updates to virus definitions, personal firewalls, browsers and other software on which the security of your computer depends.
- Monitor alerts and developments in malicious software from the Press or appropriate websites. Take appropriate action <u>immediately</u> if a patch is required for your computer.
- Consider upgrading your software to a newer version or major new release if it contains features that will enhance your confidence in the security of your arrangements
- Enable anti-virus software and personal firewalls to operate in the background all the time. Moreover, test for the presence of viruses, Trojan horse and other malicious

software on a regular basis: this vigilance should reflect the value of the software and data in your computer to your personal life.
- Remove all malicious software found – do NOT share it with anyone else
- Back up data. This requires very systematic and comprehensive back-ups. There is a wide variety of commercial software available to facilitate this process. Should the worst happen you would have access to your back-up files.

There are of course other risks to consider, such as those of an electric power surge, hardware failure (loss of the hard disk), or worse, the loss or theft of your computer.

Power supply protection devices come in a wide price range, from a simple surge arrestor to an uninterruptible power supply (UPS) containing batteries that takes over should the mains electricity be turned off. Here, expenditure should match the need and the likelihood of such an event.

Should your hard disk fail without a complete backup, there are companies specializing in data recovery. Their services also cover situations where the damage was caused by fire or water.

Losing a notebook computer containing unprotected, unencrypted data is, regrettably a common occurrence. There is little that can be done to recover the computer and prevention is definitely better than cure.

Personal matters

Security is based on two very simple rules:

---
1. TRUST NO ONE
2. NO DISCLOSURE

The protection of personal information and privacy rely strongly on a little knowledge and a lot of common sense. The following are all simple to implement and quite effective:

- Beware of downloading and running programs (games, screen savers, etc) from sources that cannot be vouched for.
- Don't give your credit card number unless the website URL is https AND the padlock is showing in the browser screen, AND the web-site is trusted
- Beware of offers that appear too good to be true – they usually are, e.g. rewards or prizes in exchange for your contact or other information.
- NEVER reply to spammers: this confirms that your address is active and read – the result is that this will become known to more spammers. Clever spammers rely on e-mail software to tell them you have read the message. You should disable your e-mail package's automatic return receipt requests.
- If the problem becomes serious, contact your ISP with copies of the spam-mail so that they can forward your complaint to the spammer's ISP.
- Use and maintain well designed User IDs and passwords – cycling criteria
- Keep copies of your user ID and password in a secure and confidential place
- Attachments are files sent together with an e-mail message. Such files can consist of text document, digital photographs or other images, computer programs and many other useful items. They can also contain malicious code. Care should be exercised at all times when dealing with attachments, even if these appear to come from a trusted source.
- If there is the slightest doubt about the legitimacy of an attachment, don't open it until you can validate with the sender that it is OK to do so.

12. RESPONDING TO A SECURITY INCIDENT

"I think we have a problem"

Something happened: You discovered that your organization's information resources have been compromised.

Scenario 1: An obvious problem, the result of a logical bomb being activated, a virus, worm or Denial of Service Attack, etc. The systems in your organization no longer work, data has been lost or corrupted and the staff is unable to work productively.

In the first instance, someone, usually on behalf of the Chief Information Officer or IT Manager will have to act quickly and effectively to contain the damage and restore operations.

In situations where information systems and facilities are critical to an organization, the only viable answer is that of having in place an Emergency Response Team of empowered and trained staff – capable of being mobilised in a very short time regardless of day of the week and time of day.

Dealing with a difficult situation is not a good time to improvise. An effective response to an incident will include six specific groups of tasks, namely, preparation, identification, containment, eradication, recovery and follow-up

In addition, it is very useful to have an emergency plan based on common sense to handle the situation in the event of an unpleasant situation. A typical emergency plan would contain steps such as:

Don't panic. Any incident raises stress levels all round. Communication and coordination become difficult and calm, particularly from senior management can help others to avoid making critical errors.

Take notes. The managers responsible for security should create a set of record-keeping forms to be used in the event that the security incident becomes a matter for a court of law. These notes may become legal evidence. Good records should focus on **W**ho, **W**hat, **W**hen and **W**here. **W**henever possible, **H**ow and **W**hy should also be part of the record.

Get help. The first person to notify is your security coordinator. The telephone directory of the organization is a vital tool and, to complement the notes mentioned above, keep notes about each person contacted and what was said.

Apply a "need to know" policy. Disclose, if you must, the details of the incident to the minimum number of people possible. Remind them that they are trusted individuals and that discretion is essential. Do not speculate.

Use trusted communications. If the computers may have been compromised, avoid using them for incident-handling discussions. Use telephones and faxes instead.

Do not send information about the incident by electronic mail, talk, chat, or news; the information may be intercepted by the attacker and used to worsen the situation. When computers are being used, encrypt all incident handling e-mail.

Contain the problem. Take all possible steps to prevent the problem from getting worse. Generally that means removing the system from the network, though keeping connections open may help to catch an intruder.

Make a backup of the affected system(s) as soon as possible. Use new, unused media. If possible make a binary, or bit-by-bit backup.

Fix the problem. Identify what went wrong if you can. Take steps to correct the deficiencies that allowed the problem to occur.

Restore normal service. After checking your backups to ensure they are not compromised, restore your system from backups and monitor the system closely to determine whether it can resume its tasks.

<u>Learn from the experience</u>. You don't want to get caught unprepared the next time.

Scenario 2: Your organization does not know that it has been attacked. This could take the form of stolen data, a defaced website, the rerouting of external traffic, unknown software such as a Trojan Horse or a back door or the defrauding of the organization.

In this scenario, the time of improper action may have preceded discovery by a substantial period of time, and many such events are discovered by chance rather than by design or audits.

Upon discovery, the CIO will have to take measures in line with a corporate policy for such matters, as it will be necessary to obtain evidence and comply with the legal requirements of digital forensics. In addition, the offending attack needs to be dealt with.

To investigate or not to investigate? That is the question.

There are no fixed and immutable rules to help decide whether or not an attack regardless of the scenario should be followed by a detailed analysis of the attack, its causes, how security was breached and subsequent reporting.

In the case of Scenario 2, it is always best that an investigation should be conducted and that the CIO should in fact take the initiative before the chief executive asks the internal or external auditors to do so.

Such an investigation should also determine if the security measures taken are consistent with the minimum requirements of the organization (the formal adoption of an international standard such as ISO 17799 would be such a minimum).

For the IT manager concerned, the best outcome of such an investigation is one that confirms reasonable measures had been taken and that the security breach could have been prevented only by measures that would have been inconsistent with the organization's assessment of threats, vulnerabilities and residual risks.

Even under the most benevolent management regime, this outcome should occur no more than twice; the first time was bad luck, and the second time a coincidence. In many organizations, a second security breach would not be considered acceptable.

The investigation may well show that the measures taken were inadequate and that the CIO or IT manager was negligent in the execution of his duties. This generally turns out to be career limiting.

If the findings reveal that the CIO or IT manager was grossly or willfully negligent this opens the possibility of legal action leading to punitive damages.

Conduct intrusion detection tests

Some 15 years ago, a leading IT journal, *Datamation*, carried on its cover the following text:

> **How good is your I.T. shop?
> Find out before your boss does.**

This message remains valid today, and in the particular case of information security, it is strongly recommended that regular and serious tests be carried out to validate security arrangements before someone else exploits any weaknesses. Such tests may include one or all of the following:
- Pre-announced tests carried out by staff
- Pre-announced tests carried out by a trusted third party
- Unannounced tests by staff and/or a trusted third party
- Intrusions detected by an unknown and thus untrusted third party (hacker)
- Security tests performed during a test of the Disaster Recovery Plan

It needs to be recognised that successful tests do not constitute a guarantee. They simply mean "so far so good".

At the end of such tests, any successful security breach regardless of its nature virus attack, Denial of Service attack, intrusion leading to access to data, or other, should be the subject of a detailed review of the technical and procedural weaknesses in the arrangements.

Have independent security audits carried out

It is a fact of life that many organizations do not conduct Information Systems and Technology audits with a frequency and scope that reflects the critical dependence they have on these technical means.

Because of such dependence, the nature of IT audits has changed dramatically in the last few years and the IT Governance Institute in the United States of America has issued what has effectively become the Open Standard for the Audit of IT, including all appropriate controls and security.

These are referred to as COBIT (Control Objectives for Information Technology) and have been widely adopted in many countries.

Similarly, ISO 17799 lends itself to form the framework for security-focused audits of Information Technology.

An organization has several choices. It can arrange for:
- Audits to be carried out by the organization's internal auditors – whenever these have adequate resources to conduct IT and, in particular, security audits
- Audits to be carried out by the organization's external auditors
- Specialised security audits to be carried out by a trusted third party
- Security audits and reviews as required for certification to ISO 17799

In the latter two cases, trust is a vital component of the audit arrangements as the auditors will, in the course of their work, have access to every detail of the security arrangements, their vulnerabilities and weaknesses. The contracts relating to such audits must include appropriate non-disclosure clauses and conditions.

Restore systems and facilities to an operating status

This action is needed to restore a compromised system to normal operation and allow staff to have access to that system again, possibly even before a full analysis is completed and all corrections are made. In this case, the risk of doing so needs to be managed and monitored, in particular focusing on continued analysis of the incident, elimination of any intruders' access, and acknowledge the vulnerability to similar types of intrusion.

This section defines steps to assist in the correction of damage, such as disconnecting any compromised systems. Details about restoring any specific business application or related service are beyond the scope of this section.

One of the purposes of a response process is to eliminate vulnerabilities that allow a security incident to occur and to return affected systems to full operational status.

The first step towards restoring a system is the determination of the requirements and timeframe for returning the system to normal operations. This cannot be achieved without the involvement of senior management.

If the system affected is mission-critical to the organization, analysis will have to continue in parallel and the system must be upgraded as soon as possible, accepting that until then the system is vulnerable to another incident of the same type. Increasing the level of system monitoring would help identify the emergence of another incident.

Any such restoration must use the latest trusted backup of user data from backup media known to be secure, as the incident may

have altered user data and application program areas. Examples where this may occur include:
- The installation by an intruder of back doors to provide future access. For example, an intruder might install a program in a local user directory that is called each time the user logs in, providing an unprotected login shell that can be accessed by anyone via the Internet.
- The modification of user data to sabotage the user's work. For example, an intruder makes small unnoticed changes to spreadsheets. Depending on how the spreadsheets are used, this can cause minor to major damage.

Users must be asked to check for unexpected changes to their files or data and be warned about the risk of compromise.

All executable and binary files residing in user areas should be handled in the same way as system executables and binary files. If no authenticated validation is available, they must be reinstalled from the original distribution media.

As the process continues, only those services required by the users of the system should be restored, i.e. NOT all available services.

The restored system should now be validated through tests such that the results can be compared with the results of prior tests.

Once a system has been compromised, particularly by an intruder, this becomes well known in the hacker community, and as a result, the system may become a target for future attacks. Improved monitoring may reveal new attacks more easily and provide the opportunity to defeat the attacker.

A comprehensive description of these practices, together with implementation details for selected technologies, is available on the Website of CERT (Computer Emergency Response Team, at Carnegie Mellon University) at URL:
"http://www.cert.org/security-improvement/practices/p051.html"

Have robust and tested disaster recovery and continuity plans

If systems cannot be restored quickly enough to meet operational requirements, it may be necessary to invoke contingency plans and disaster recovery arrangements.

The traditional practice of Disaster Recovery originated with the centralised data center and makes provision for similar facilities to be available at a separate location in the event that a data center becomes unusable as a result of fire, flooding, hurricane, etc.

Depending on the criticality of the services provided by the data center, the time to recover information systems and facilities would normally range between several days (cold site recovery) and minutes (hot site recovery). There is a substantial difference in the cost of such arrangements.

As the number of technologies in a data center and in an organization's building increases, so does the complexity of disaster recovery.

The logistics of moving people, data and software to another location, communicating the situation to managers, end users and other interested parties, and getting things back to work are challenging. Detailed documentation must communicated to all parties likely to be involved and, most important of all, regularly tested. Failure to test Disaster Recovery plans invariably results in having to resolve serious problems while already in crisis mode.

Global connectivity and the growing criticality of information systems and technology are gradually forcing organizations to plan for shorter and shorter recovery times, which result in greater complexity and higher cost.

In addition, it is now not enough to simply recover information systems, it is also essential to guarantee some level of business continuity – the availability of facilities for employees and managers to continue to perform essential tasks in a place other than their offices, which may not be accessible or available.

What happens when Information Systems and Technology activities have been outsourced?

Outsourcing, the contractual transfer of responsibility for the performance of some tasks or services has been a major trend in Information Technology over the course of the last decade.

Given that IT requires a growing number of staff with specialised skills and experience, many organizations choose to rely on others, whose core expertise is in the area of IT service delivery, even if this appears more expensive than an in-house arrangements.

Outsourcing contracts need to be very specific as to the responsibilities of both parties, in particular with regard to information security and the actions to be taken in the case of a security incident.

Outsourcing does not absolve the organization from its responsibilities concerning information security, in particular, defining the value of the assets to be protected, creating an awareness of information security issues with their employees, contractors, etc.

It is recommended that the contract with an outsourcing company should make provision for the ability to audit the outsourcer by the client's chosen auditors.

Whilst responsibility for implementing a disaster recovery plan rests with the outsourcing vendor, arrangements for business continuity remain firmly with the organization.

Digital forensics

This short section expands on the introduction to this topic made earlier.

If the reader is fortunate, this topic will be of no more than academic interest. In practice, executives are increasingly likely to need to avail themselves of digital forensics, the study of information technologies as they relate to the law, and defined by stating that "Digital Forensics deal with the preservation, identification, extraction and documentation of computer evidence".

Who needs to use digital forensics? In practice anyone who needs to handle a case of fraud, sabotage, industrial espionage or other offences.

Who needs evidence: Executives and managers, criminal and civil lawyers, insurance companies, law enforcement officials and individuals. Such evidence must be obtained and secured in such a way as to retain its legal value.

Evidence can be <u>visible</u> – in the form of unencrypted stored data in a computer or data intercepted as it flows through a network and which is not hidden. There are other more complex forms of evidence:

<u>Visible-Invisible</u> evidence: information that is deliberately hidden through the use of passwords or encryption or information hidden in another file. Steganography is an example of the tools used to hide data.

In an investigation, logs, also part of the Visible Invisible evidence, may additionally show activity at unusual times or missing sequential numbers.

<u>Invisible-Invisible</u> evidence falls in to two categories:

That which has not been hidden by an individual but hidden by the system itself, as is the case with Windows temporary files, swap files, Internet temporary files, etc

That which has been hidden deliberately, which includes files erased (as opposed to deleted) by a person as deleted files can usually be recovered.

Securing the evidence requires a good knowledge of all applicable legislation. Invariably, there are several common elements in such legislation including:
- The documentation of the time, date and circumstances of the seizure
- The collection of all physical evidence associated with the event (Post-It Notes ™, desk calendars, notebooks, manuals, contents of waste baskets, floppy disks)
- Labeling all evidence in a clear manner
- Discovering **all** files (normal, deleted, password protected, encrypted, hidden)
- Recording all serial numbers, documentation of system layout, etc)
- Transferring all items under investigation to a secure location taking particular care not to expose them to electromagnetic interference, and restricting access to this location
- Creating a secure set of no less than two copies of everything using disk imaging techniques, keeping one copy in an evidence container

and many more such activities. The key point is that unless evidence has been collected, kept, analyzed, disclosed, etc., in full compliance with the applicable legislation, it risks being dismissed by a court of law.

It is strongly recommended that both the internal auditors of the organization as well as legal counsel be closely involved with these processes.

Other considerations

These are early days in the management of information security. Things are not likely to become simpler. Amongst the emerging headaches facing CIOs and IT Managers are:
- The emerging world of mobile computing and tele-working and the problem of "junior" using Father's access to the corporate network from home to *"download interesting stuff"* from the Web,

- The proliferation of small, easy to lose, portable devices containing corporate data and documents and possibly automated mechanisms for accessing corporate networks (a large number of software packages and applications will offer to "remember your password")
- The potential for malicious software to become seriously damaging, by deleting or corrupting corporate document repositories, databases or systems data
- The explosive growth of documents and other forms of information in digital form whereby storage (as well as backups and disaster recovery) become a significant technical and operational challenge.

13. OBSERVATIONS AND EXPERIENCES

The following observations are presented in an effort to help establish a partial checklist of essential actions in cases of security breaches.

Liability

The possibility of legal liability after a security breach should be a major concern for any person responsible for managing information security in an organisation.

A review or post-mortem should always take place after a security incident. This could be carried out by the security team itself but, in serious cases, auditors and external investigators may need be involved.

However, should the review find that the responsible manager failed to exercise due diligence, this opens the possibility of being sued in a court of law for damages. Worse still, should the review indicate that the manager acted negligently, or that there are grounds to suspect fraud, sabotage or aiding and abetting crime, and should the organisation decide to pursue this matter through the law, the case could be referred to a civil or a criminal court.

Monitoring and searches

The legal situation concerning the right of an employer to monitor the work of an employee through, for example, scanning e-mail for offensive language or inappropriate attachments, and tracking the employee's mailing routes through the World Wide Web, differs from country to country.

This raises complex issues when there is no indication of malicious intent as the rights of the employer are counterbalanced by the right to privacy of an individual while working for an employer. When there is adequate reason to believe that the employee's behaviour may be detrimental to the interests of the employer, monitoring and searches may be conducted and it is recommended that the organisation's legal counsel be consulted first.

Theft or misuse of personal information

In most countries, an individual has little recourse, other than insurance, if someone in cyberspace steals and misuses personal information. Such an offence may range from a simple theft of credit card information to a full identity theft.

Should somebody steal an e-mail account and use it inappropriately, the legitimate owner would have great difficulty proving that this was somebody else's initiative unless a detailed forensic examination is conducted which, in turn, would require the evidence to be available.

Trust vis-à-vis security auditors

Whenever security auditors are brought in from outside an organisation, there is a major issue of trust to consider as by the time the audit is completed, the auditors will have an in-depth knowledge of the security arrangements and practices of an organisation, its vulnerabilities and shortcomings and, in particular, detailed information about the technologies used, how these are configured and how their audit succeeded in penetrating these defences (most quality security auditors do manage to get past security arrangements).

However reputable a security audit company, or a security consultant, the issue remains that the best security auditors are in fact ethical hackers. How ethical is ethical?

Social engineering as an aid to cyber-crime

Openness and assumed trust characterise many organisations. It is therefore not all that difficult for a person with malicious intent to acquire privileged information just by asking for it.

Example: a visitor to an organisation may have unsupervised access to a telephone. Calling an employee, particularly a new recruit, from an internal extension number and pretending to be the Help Desk, the visitor may be able to acquire a valid user ID and password by saying that it is necessary to confirm the setup.

Similarly, a person can impersonate a maintenance technician and plug in a notebook computer into the corporate network. This is easier to do than it seems, due to the fact that, in large organisations the supposed practice that all visitors should be escorted at all times is often relaxed. At this point, all firewalls and security arrangements have become worthless.

National and international legislation on cyber-crime

Effective legislation to cover cyber-crime in its many forms is considered to cover three main areas:
- The protection of intellectual property, including software
- The protection of individual privacy in cyberspace
- The definition of deterrents and the possibility of prosecution for cyber-crime offences.

> **Does it sound daunting? It is.**
> **Do you really have any choice?**

THE ACTION PLAN

The bad news unfortunately gets worse. The lack of awareness about the scope and impact of information insecurity, and the absence of an effective ICT security strategy in many organizations, pales into insignificance in the face of the unconscionable gaps in the legislation on this issue.

The gaps in legislation are easily exploited by the cyber-criminal in the full knowledge that punishment, if ever caught, would only be minor.

Proper legislation would have to lie in two distinct areas – national legislation to cover issues of internal responsibility and liability, and international legislation relating to the inter-state aspects of jurisdiction, ownership, responsibility, and liability. Both are relatively absent at present.

14. BEST PRACTICES AND STANDARDS

Cyberspace as a Frontierland

Cyberspace in the early 21st Century can be looked upon as a Frontierland. In human history there have been many such Frontierlands as a result of exploration and/or innovation.

The characteristics that define a Frontierland include:

<u>Uncharted territory</u> – there are no detailed maps showing boundaries or landmarks – those venturing into Frontierland need to think and behave as explorers.

<u>Unclear or undefined ownership</u> – many Frontierlands have been claimed in the name of a ruler, whose explorers first stumbled by design or by luck upon such lands. Others are fought for until ownership, or at least control, is achieved by a dominance established by the most powerful contender

Lack of legislation – an orderly and fair society does not emerge until the Frontierland has been explored, settled and disputed for some time. Disputes and other matters dealt with through a legal code elsewhere are handled more pragmatically in Frontierland. It may be rough justice but that's all there is.

Adventurers – The above three characteristics can be seen as a problem by those whose reference framework is one of an orderly society and the rule of law. They are also seen as opportunities by those willing to take risks. Indeed, many adventurers in past Frontierlands became highly successful, and are often remembered with reverence. Those who failed, however, have been forgotten long ago.

Some Frontierlands are readily recognized as such and quite well known through literature and cinema, such as the North American "Wild West" of the mid-19th century. However, if the above characteristics are accepted as valid, humanity is still grappling with other Frontierlands, such as those of Nuclear, Biological and Chemical material, and is beginning to be concerned with emerging Frontierlands including Genetics, Nano-engineering, and Robotics.

Like all technologies, these can be used to benefit humanity and make a better world, and yet also have the potential to be used as weapons. Chemical weapons were used in World War I and nuclear bombs were first used in World War II. Work towards treaties on the use of such weapons, remains in progress and not every country is ready to ratify the treaties that emerge.

Information Security also falls in this category, although as an emerging issue as the technologies of chemical, bacteriological and nuclear weapons have been in existence many years before cyberspace and their potential as weapons of mass destruction much easier to understand than the potential of information to disrupt society.

It needs to be recognised that new Frontierlands of this kind will continue to emerge and, given the worldwide acceleration of technical and scientific innovation, they will do so at shorter intervals than hitherto. Philosophers and other writers considering this matter have already identified genetics, nano-technologies and robotics as likely to bring new ethical and control problems of a very complex nature.

Approaches to survive in Frontierland

As our knowledge and understanding of Frontierland increase, they make available better charts of the territory. Each Frontierland will have its distinctive charts and what works for one Frontierland will, in all likelihood, be unsuitable for a new Frontierland.

Frontierland becomes fit for civil society in a number of steps. For security in cyber-space these steps are three: Best Practices, Standards and Legislation.

Best practices for managing information security

For managing Information Security, these first charts consist of widely accepted best practices.

These often start as extensions to previous tried and tested practices. In many areas these remain as "best practices" and are never standardized. One specific cyber-space example can be found in the practices of "disaster recovery" and "business continuity":

As information and communications technology play a more critical role in the day-to-day activities of an organization, it becomes necessary to make arrangements for the event that these technologies become inoperational for a period of time greater than the organization can accept without major disruption to its activities.

Financial institutions, banks, airlines, critical infrastructures (electricity, water) have plans that allow them to resume operations in the case of a major ICT problem within, at most, a few hours. The original plans were designed to cope with catastrophic events in a computer room or data center (flooding, hurricanes, fire, major hardware failures).

The emergence of cyberspace and the possibility of remote sabotage, denial of service attacks or similar events, have required that disaster recovery plans be updated and extended to deal with a new collection of disruptive events.

There are many sources of best practices, some free of charge and others at low cost, developed by practitioners and professional associations. A list of such sources is included in the references. Nevertheless, the following deserve specific mention here:

- **ITIL Security World:** The Information Technology Infrastructure Library, originally produced by the U.K. Central Computing and Telecommunications Agency's, now an automous agency, in extensive use around the world;
- **COBIT:** The Control Objectives for Information Technology guidelines published by the Information Systems Audit and Control Association (ISACA) are very highly regarded.
- **SANS:** the Systems And Network Security Institute professional training association (www.sans.org) has several books on offer (priced at around 30 US dollars each) on many technical aspects of information security and run frequent training courses in the US and elsewhere;
- **CASPR:** the Commonly Accepted Security Practices and Recommendations (www.caspr.org). The owners of this website intended to provide comprehensive best practices on information security in the year 2002 but in mid-August 2002 the website was disappointingly empty, merely indicating the intention to have such documents "soon"

The international community has a great opportunity to launch a project to seek the agreement of the above, and similar, organizations to select, translate and disseminate these best practices in languages other than English.

Having access to best practices and applying them systematically are fundamentally different things. There are two complementary approaches to validating how well these are applied: Tests and Audits.

For activities such as disaster recovery and the robustness of defences against penetration, tests are the only effective method to determine whether things will work when called upon. Although such tests are complex and usually disruptive, there really is no alternative.

Standards for information security

When the charts become sufficiently detailed and incorporate the experience of many parties, they can be formalized into "official" charts referred to as standards.

Standards play an important role in the transformation of a Frontierland into an orderly society, where the rules of interaction are defined and widely applied. For example the technical and operating standards defined by the Internet Engineering Task Force (www.ietf.org) enabled the Internet to become a global network in a relatively short time. Access to an Internet Café or a contract with an Internet Service Provider, then become the "passport" that grants an individual access to this portion of Cyber-space.

There are four sources of standards and recommendations:

1. The International Standards Organization (ISO), often in collaboration with International Organizations such as the International Telecommunications Union (ITU) or with national standards organizations such as the British Standards Institute.

Examples:
- ISO 13335: A five part set of guidelines for the management of information security precedes ISO 17799 by some 4 years
- ISO 15408: Common Criteria for information security evaluation (see also the website at

www.commoncriteria.org) - this standard is downloadable free of charge
- ISO 17799: Code of Practice for the Management of Information Security
- ITU recommendation X. 273: Open Systems Interconnection, network layer security protocol
- ITU recommendation X. 509: Authentication framework (relates to digital certificates and public key encryption infrastructure)

2. Other national and regional organizations:
- NATO Orange and Red books for trusted computer systems (also the U.S. Department of Defense Rainbow Series on trusted computer systems) first produced in the late 1980s.
- Other bodies working on standardization include ETSI (European Telecommunications Standardization Institute), under the auspices of the Council of Europe.
- An appropriate example of a national standards body is the National Institute of Standards and Technology of the U.S. Government and its Computer Security Resource Centre (http://csrc.nist.gov)

3. Professional associations, such as the Institution of Electrical and Electronic Engineers (IEEE), based in the United States but with a worldwide membership and the Internet Engineering Task Force (IETF), also with a worldwide membership,

Examples:
- IEEE 802.10: Standard for Interoperable Local Network Security (SILS)
- IETF: IPSEC working group
- IETF: SAAG (Security Area Advisory Group)

4. Vendor associations such as ECMA, the European Computer Manufacturers Association or vendors whose products in such ubiquitous use that their architecture and software become the dominant technology and as such, *de-facto* standards

Examples:

- ECMA TC29/TGS: Security Aspects of Documents
- ECMA TC32/TG9: Security in Open Systems (authentication)
- Microsoft's Windows family of products, Internet Explorer and Outlook Express
- Netscape Navigator

15. CURRENT NATIONAL AND REGIONAL LEGISLATION

The important role of information and communications technologies in today's society is no longer underestimated. These systems play critical roles in financial transactions – SWIFT (Society for worldwide inter-bank fund transfers) moves trillions of US dollars per day in electronic form; critical infrastructures are highly computerized and the amount of confidential personal information held in electronic form is just prodigious.

The protection of society against breaches of information security can no longer be a simple matter of trust: it has become a legal issue. However, technology advances faster than legislators' ability to formulate, validate and put in place adequate laws and regulations. This implies that we shall continue to live in Frontierland for a considerable time.

The following portions of this chapter will indicate the completely fragmented and disparate nature of the initiatives that have been taken by different actors in the area of legislation.

Private Sector initiatives

A number of non-governmental organizations have taken great interest in the matter, despite the clear fact that legislation falls within the purview of legislators and governments alone. Among the more prominent of these private sector organizations are:
- The International Chamber of Commerce (ICC).
- The Global Business Dialogue on Electronic Commerce (GBDE).
- The Information Technology Association of America (ITAA).

- The World Information Technology and Services Alliance (WITSA).
- The Global Internet Project (GIP).
- The Global Information Infrastructure Commission (GIIC).

Some of these organizations have established working groups and task forces to work in a focused fashion on the question of the gaps in legislation.

As this whole subject of legislation moves forward, these and other parts of the private sector and civil society will have to be brought into the negotiating loop in the interest of durable laws.

National legislation

Many countries have been introducing national legislation on all or at least some of the aspects concerning either cyber-crime or cyber- security. Almost all of these are developed countries. Developing countries are noticeably absent.

In the case of laws relating to crimes against computer content and computer systems, examples of the more important legislative actions are:
- Australia – Cybercrime Act 2001.
  through <http://search.aph.gov.au>
- Canada – Sections 342.1 and 430(1.1) of the Criminal Code. http://lois.justice.gc.ca/en/C-46/39387.html
- Japan – Unauthorised Computer Access Law 1999. http://www.meti.go.jp/english/report/data/gMI1102e.htm
- UK – Computer Misuse Act 1990. <http://www.bailii.org/uk/legis/num_act/cma1990204/>
- USA – Computer Fraud and Abuse Act, as amended in 2001. http://www.usdoj.gov/criminal/cybercrime/1030_new.html

In the case of laws relating to crimes against communications systems (wire-tapping, privacy, etc.), the more important legislative actions are:
- Canada – Sections 183 and 196 of the Criminal Code. <http://lois.justice.gc.ca/en/C-46/38885.htm>
- Germany – Telecommunications Acts. <http://www.netlaw.de/gesetze/tkg.htm>
- Italy – Section 266 of the Criminal Code.
- Japan – Law on Communication Interception during Criminal Investigations.
- UK – Regulation of Investigative Powers Act. <http://www.legislation.hmso.gov.uk/acts/acts2000/20000023.htm>
- USA – Electronic Communications Privacy Act. <http://www.cybercrime.gov>

It is to be noted that there is relatively little legislation on issues relating to fraud, money-laundering, identity theft, etc., though the United States does have laws that address parts of the problem.

Multi-national and regional legislation

There are three major initiatives that need to be studied carefully:
- The Council of Europe Convention on Cyber-crime of 2001
- The G-8 Lyon Group recommendations of 1999 to combat trans-national organized crime
- The OAS Final Report of 2000 on the two meetings of their Attorneys General and Ministers of Justice and Interior.

The Council of Europe Convention on Cyber-crime

The major event of 2001 was the emergence of the Council of Europe Convention on Cyber-Crime. This convention addresses unauthorised access, system interference and sabotage, data interception and data modification, data theft and misuse and aiding and abetting cyber criminals.

Its three primary groups of provisions are designed to enable signatory nations to implement computer-related criminal law standards. These three groups of provisions cover:
- The outlawing of unauthorised computer intrusion, the release of malicious code, the use of computers to commit acts which are already crimes (e.g. fraud),
- The development of procedures to capture and retrieve on-line and other information by issuing "retention orders"
- The cooperation between national governments to share electronic evidence

Reaction 1: Signature and ratification of the Convention

By mid 2002, 33 States had signed, but not ratified, the Council of Europe Convention on Cyber-crime: These included 29 of the 44 members of the Council and four non-members who participated in the negotiations (the United States of America, Canada, Japan and South Africa).

The 29 Council Members that have signed the convention are: Albania, Armenia, Austria, Belgium, Bulgaria, Croatia, Cyprus, Estonia, Finland, France, Germany, Greece, Hungary, Iceland, Ireland, Italy, Macedonia, Malta, Moldova, the Netherlands, Norway, Poland, Portugal, Romania, Spain, Sweden, Switzerland, Ukraine and the United Kingdom.

The convention will enter into force when it has been ratified by five states, of which at least three must be members of the Council. The EU hopes to complete the ratification process by the middle of 2003.

Reaction 2: Misgivings

There have been many concerns expressed about the Council of Europe's Convention on Cyber-crime. Among them:

The Council is understood to be drafting an additional protocol for the convention that would treat xenophobic or racist acts committed in cyberspace as criminal offences. However, the

United States indicated that such a protocol would be in contravention with its legislation on the freedom of speech.

A pending area is a proposed extension to the convention to permit the interception and decoding of electronic messages between individuals suspected of terrorist activity.

Another area of criticism of the convention is that more countries would have to sign and ratify the convention and abide by its mandates in order for it to be an effective deterrent. Critics note that none of the countries that have signed the convention so far are "problem countries" in which cyber-criminals can act with impunity. It is known that hackers and other attackers route their traffic through portals and facilities in countries that have not signed the convention.

Civil liberties groups have also expressed concern that the convention undermines individual rights to privacy and extends the surveillance powers of the signatory governments.

Critics in the United States indicate that the provisions of the convention are incompatible with current U.S. law.

Critics in Europe are concerned that the provisions of the convention allow the transfer of personal data to countries outside Europe, notably the United States and express the belief that the U.S. has less protective legislation regarding the use of such information and that it also may enable "foreign" countries to issue warrants seeking evidence and extradite and prosecute foreign nationals for cyber-crimes.

In addition, lobbyists acting on behalf of business and consumer groups are concerned that the provisions of the CoE Convention could increase the cost of e-business, delay or impede the development of security technologies, limit the export of encryption products, and reduce consumer confidence in e-commerce.

G-8 initiatives

The Lyon Group established by the G-8 in 1995 has worked on 40 recommendations to combat trans-national organized crime. One of these recommendations calls on members to "review their laws to ensure that abuses of modern technology are criminalized".

In 2002 the G-8 considered (but did not adopt) nine non-binding principles for information security:
- The creation of emergency watch and warning networks.
- The sharing of critical infrastructure information between the public and private sectors.
- Legal systems to ensure that such sharing of information is actually possible.
- Legal systems to enable the sharing of such information with third countries.
- The creation of secure and stable governmental communications for situations of emergencies.
- The mapping of critical infrastructures, and their inter-dependence.
- Legal systems to ensure against data destruction.
- The coordination of work among all stakeholders.
- Training exercises to enhance response capabilities.

Organisation of American States initiatives

The OAS established an inter-governmental group of experts on cyber-crime in 1999. The Final Report of the Group can be seen at:
<http://www.oas.org/juridico/english/present/finalrep.doc>

16. GLOBAL INTERNATIONAL LEGISLATION

The development of truly global international legislation is advancing much too slowly and in a fragmented manner. Global international legislation is needed because cyber-space does not have the same geopolitical borders as nation states and cyber-crime does not require a physical presence at the scene of crime.

There must be no non-signatories, as any loophole will be immediately exploited by the cyber-criminal and cyber-terrorist.

There are two interesting older initiatives to address this issue, and much can be learnt from both.

The first can be seen in a document entitled, "International review of criminal policy. United Nations Manual on the prevention and control of computer-related crime" is. The original is a document of the UN Office in Vienna, Center for Social Development and Humanitarian Affairs, under the title "International Review of Criminal Policy - Nos. 43 and 44" of 1994.

This manual is widely quoted in websites dealing with cyber-law. It calls for further international work and presents a good statement of the problem. Its two final paragraphs are quoted below in italics, as they remain relevant and as actionable as they were when first written. They state:

> *"295. At the international level, further activities could be undertaken, including the following:*
>
> *1. Within regional groups or associations, conducting comparative analyses of substantive and procedural law relating to computer crime;*
>
> *2. Attempting to harmonize substantive and procedural law among the States of a region by developing guidelines, model law or agreements;*
>
> *3. When negotiating or reviewing treaties on extradition, mutual assistance or transfer of proceedings, whether bilateral or multilateral, addressing the following issues, taking into account human rights, including privacy rights, and the sovereignty of States:*
>
> *4. Ensuring a jurisdictional base for the prosecution of trans-border, computer-related crime and enacting mechanisms for resolving jurisdictional conflicts;*

> 5. Imposing obligations to extradite or prosecute offenders;
>
> 6. Facilitating mutual assistance, particularly regarding synchronized law enforcement, transborder search and seizure and the interception of communications.

"296. To ensure that human rights principles, privacy rights and international legal principles are effectively balanced, model treaties on criminal matters, such as those developed by the United Nations, can provide valuable guidelines. The implementation of security and crime prevention measures should be concomitant with technological development. The time to act is now."

The second initiative to create a formal framework for cyber-space was put forward in 1994 by the Progress Freedom Foundation. This is a document entitled "Cyber-space and the American Dream. A Magna Carta for the Knowledge Age" authored by Esther Dyson, George Gilder, George Keyworth and Alvin Toffler. The document can be found at the following URL: <http://www.pff.org/position.html>

Despite its publication so many years ago, no further discussion of this document could be found in the World Wide Web.

Some work has been done by different elements of the United Nations System, like the United Nations Conference on Trade and Development (UNCTAD), the World Intellectual Property Organization (WIPO), the World Trade Organization (WTO), etc, but no truly coordinated global work exists at present.

The United Nations General Assembly has several resolutions dealing with its desire to see progress on this issue. Among these are:
- Resolutions 55/63 and 56/121 on Combatting the Criminal Misuse of Information Technology, which noted the value of the G-8 principles, and urged states to take these principles into account.

- Resolutions 53/70, 54/79, 55/28, and 56/19, all of which call on Member States of the United Nations to promote the multi-lateral "consideration of existing and potential threats in the field of information security, as well as possible measures to limit the threats emerging in this field".

17. THE LAW OF CYBER-SPACE

It is clear that the current national and international legislation is completely insufficient to address the scope and complexity of the subject of cyber-threats and cyber-attack. A determined effort has consequently to be made to identify the shortcomings in existing legislation, and to draft and adopt a comprehensive Law of Cyber-Space. Such a Law of Cyber-Space would have to address the following issues, among others:
- Definition of cyber-space
- Sovereignty and jurisdiction
- Right to access
- Cyber-hooliganism
- Cyber-crime
- Cyber-terrorism
- Cyber-war
- National security
- Standards of evidence
- Intellectual property
- Software, including encryption
- Data protection
- Malicious code
- Electronic commerce
- Telecommunications regulation
- Obscene publications and related matters
- Civil liberties and right to privacy
- Anonymity
- Regulatory and investigative powers
- International cooperation mechanisms
- Trans-national extradition
- Treaty secretariat

Obviously all this cannot be done within the framework of national legislation alone. Different countries have different legal systems, standards and rules, and therefore harmonization would be almost impossible. Some countries might opt to stay out of the system, and would then become "offshore" havens for cyber-crime and cyber-terrorism.

It cannot be done in regional forums either, as the problem has global dimensions that cannot be defined in regional terms.

The manner in which cyber-space envelops the globe, and manages to freely cross borders without let or hindrance, makes it absolutely essential that the parameters of the future Law of Cyber-Space will have to be developed and negotiated in a global forum for a global consensus on a global problem.

As the only truly universal international organisation that we have today, the United Nations can provide the broadest and most neutral and legitimate platform for bringing together governments and other key stakeholders to undertake this effort. Only this institution can provide the forum for discussion and debate on the complexities of the subject, and coalesce the expertise that exists around the world for a proper drafting of relevant legislation that can fill the existing and growing void in cyber-law.

It has done it before, in the nearest equivalent to cyber-space, when the United Nations negotiated and agreed on a Law of the Seas. That took almost a decade of negotiations, but the end-result was worthy of the time spent, and the consensus has withstood the passage of time.

A complication arises from the fact that both the Private Sector and Civil Society have major stakes in these negotiations. Since the United Nations is essentially an inter-governmental organisation, the question is how its Member States will adequately incorporate the interests of the Private Sector and Civil Society in the processes for the development and negotiation of a Law of Cyber-Space.

As the United Nations gains experience in building relationships with the Private Sector and Civil Society, innovative ways and means can be devised to ensure the full engagement of all key stakeholders in cyber-space, in a process whose outcome would be mutually beneficial, and which would create a solid foundation and a conducive environment for the positive use of cyber-space for the economic and social development of all countries.

In the case of earlier negotiations, for example on the Chemical Weapons Convention, government negotiators were able to ensure that they correctly represented not only their own interests, but also the interests of the chemical industry at large. So, it can be done.

What is evident is that the passage of time will only complicate the issues further, as individuals and organizations and even states stake out processes and procedures in cyber-space that are reminiscent of the old Frontierlands. Procrastination will certainly not resolve the problem by itself.

So, let us roll up our sleeves and embark on the task of developing, drafting, negotiating and adopting a Law of Cyber-Space before it is too late.

The longer we wait, the harder it will get.

RECOMMENDATIONS

Despite the complexity of this subject of Information Insecurity, there are some logical actions that would help alleviate the problems that can be caused otherwise. These can be implemented without too much difficulty. Their non-implementation would certainly create major problems all round. These recommendations are:

Recommendation No: 1 - Become aware of the problem.
While it is true that the nooks and crannies of the Information Revolution are dark and deep, and that they are constantly changing, that cannot in any way justify the widespread ignorance about the parameters of the problem. So each individual and organisation has an obligation to read and think through the problem. The greater the awareness, the easier the implementation of solutions.

Recommendation No: 2 – Devise an information security strategy.
Think this through yourself and with colleagues. Look around at how the problem is being addressed by others. Then adapt all the ideas to fit into your own set-up. Because the goal posts are shifting all the time as the technology changes and the attackers become bolder and more knowledgeable, re-evaluate your strategy frequently even if you have not apparently been the target of a cyber-attack.

Recommendation No: 3 – Implement some simpler remedial procedures immediately.
While many of the solutions are complex, and may require professional help, some are fairly simple, and if not already in place, need to be implemented immediately in any set-up, whether that of an individual home, a small business, or a large organisation. These include actions like the implementation of firewalls, the regular changing of passwords, the correct management of cookies, etc. Making a list of what can be done without outside help would reduce the problem to chewable proportions.

Recommendation No: 4 – Seek professional help without delay.
While some simple solutions are being implemented internally, some stronger fare is of course necessary, particularly in the case of governments and large organizations whose complex operations are matched by equally complex vulnerabilities. That will need professional help and advice from external auditors, specialized and experienced information consultants, ethical hackers, etc. A start should be made by contacting trustworthy professionals for advice.

Recommendation No: 5 – Adopt international standards and other best practices.
International standards like ISO 17799, and other tried and tested best practices can be of great help in securing your systems from external threats. The United Nations can be of much help in collecting and disseminating such best practices to all Member States.

Recommendation No: 6 – Identify the gaps in national legislation.
A correct understanding of national legislation is vital, not only to know its details, but also to identify its gaps. The "other side" will be doing just that also. You level the playing field by making the same degree of effort. The greater the awareness about gaps in legislation, the greater the chances that these will be duly addressed by legislators.

Recommendation No: 7 – Encourage the United Nations to embark urgently on a Law of Cyber-Space.
The almost complete absence of international law on this subject has created a phenomenal vacuum. The task of bringing together all stakeholders, and then developing, negotiating, drafting, and adopting a comprehensive and consensus Law of Cyber-Space will not be easy, and may take a fair amount of effort and time. Member States of the United Nations, and its Secretariat, need to start work on this urgently.

REFERENCES

1. The story of writing, by Andrew Robinson, Thames & Hudson, 1995

2. Codes, ciphers and secret writing, by Martin Gardner, Dover Books, 1984

3. The Victorian Internet, by Tom Standage, Orion Books, 1998

4. The Law of the Seas, United Nations. (http://www.un.org/Depts/los/index.htm)

5. The Association of Certified Fraud Examiners (http://www.cfenet.com)

6. Computer Economics Inc. (http://www.computereconomics.com)

7. Council of Europe Convention on Cyber-crime (October 2001) (http://www.coe.int)

8. United Nations Crime and Justice Information Network. (http://www.uncjin.org)

9. Hacktivism: An emerging threat to diplomacy by Dorothy E. Denning (http://cs.www.georgetown.edu/~denning/publications.html)

10. Hiding crimes in cyberspace, by Dorothy E. Denning and William E. Baugh, Jr. Information, Communication and Society, Vol. 2, No. 3, Autumn 1999.

11. Information Warfare and Security, Dorothy E. Denning, Addison-Wesley, Dec 1998

12. ISO 17799, Code of Practice for the Management of Information Security. International Standards Organisation, Geneva. (http://www.iso.ch/)

13. Cyber-war, cyber-crime and cyber-terrorism: a bibliographic essay by Jason Barkham. The American Society of International Law.

14. Cyber Terrorism and Information Warfare, Threats and Responses, by Yonah Alexander and Michael S. Sweetnam, 1999

15. Information Warfare, Time to Prepare, by Bruce Berkowitz, Issues in Science and Technology, Winter 2000. http://www.nap.edu/issues/17.2/berkowitz.htm

16. Innovation, Cyberwar, Combat on the Web, by Charles Bickers. Far-Eastern Economic Review, August 16, 2001, http://cathess.net.ac.uk/risks

17. Aspects of cyberspace law. Law Library of Georgetown University. http://ll.georgetown.edu/intl/guides/cyberspace/index.html

18. Cybercrime: An International Problem for Every Lawyer, Business and Country, American Bar Association, August 2002

APPENDIX 1

USEFUL WEBSITES

This selection of web-sites makes no attempt to be comprehensive. The inclusion of vendors or other commercial entities does not constitute an endorsement of their products or services. Web-sites relating to hacking, where to procure hacker tools, how to design malicious code, or to other activities of a potentially illegal nature, have all been deliberately excluded.

The websites in this appendix have been grouped in the following alphabetic categories:
- Activism and Hacktivism
- Alerts, incident tracking and reporting
- Auditing and e-fraud
- Cyberlaw
- International organisations
- Miscellaneous
- Security and encryption
- Security mailing lists
- Security portals
- Security standards
- Reference sites
- Vendor websites
- Virus hoaxes
- Virus information

The reader is encouraged to search the Web to obtain pertinent information on a wide range of other topics such as legislation, civil liberties and privacy, and other topics discussed in this book.

ACTIVISM AND HACKTIVISM

http://www.gn.apc.org/pmhp/ehippies/
The Electro-hippies are not hackers per se. Instead they promote civil disobedience and electronic sit-ins (WTO was one of their targets) through denial of service attacks, etc

http://www.thehacktivist.com/
Website devoted to Electronic Civil Disobedience

http://www.thing.net/~rdom/ecd/ecd.html
Topics of civil disobedience.

ALERTS, INCIDENT TRACKING AND REPORTING

http://www.attrition.org/
A web site for the collection, dissemination and distribution of information about computer security. It is especially known as the largest mirror of web site defacements.

http://cve.mitre.org/
A web site with a database of standardised names for Common Vulnerabilities and Exposures in information systems. Becoming widely referenced in the industry when referring to recognised vulnerabilities.

http://www.htcn.org/
The High Tech Crimes Network – a somewhat complex home page leads into valuable information, training and testing facilities, conferences and technology issues.

AUDITING AND E-FRAUD

http://www.isaca.org/
The Information Systems and Control Association and Foundation. The guidelines and framework for the Control Objectives for Information Technology (COBIT) can be downloaded from this website

http://www.isc2.org/
The International Information Systems Security Certification Consortium.

http://www.giac.org/
The Global Information Assurance Certification related to the SANS institute mentioned above under standards and best practices

http://www.securityauditor.net/
Developers of a software product (COBRA) to support risk analysis, self-evaluation and compliance in the framework of ISO 17799

http://www.auditnet.org/
A website dealing primarily with audit matters, including security audits.

http://www.merchantfraudsquad.com/
A not-for profit organization set up to assist merchants with fraud situations.

http://www.ifccfbi.gov/
The website of the Internet Fraud Complaint Centre.

http://www.usdoj.gov/criminal/cybercrime/index.html
Website of the Computer Crime and Intellectual Property Section of the Criminal Division of the U.S. Department of Justice. It has a good section on international matters.

CYBERLAW

There are many websites, the majority in academic circles dealing with emerging cyberlaw legislation. The selection below is suggested as a starting point

http://www.coe.int
The website of the Council of Europe. Within this site, but without a direct link, is the Convention on Cybercrime signed in 2001

http://nsi.org/
The website of the United States of America National Security Institute lists legislation proposed or approved by the U.S. Congress as well as counter-terrorism legislation covering cyberspace.

http://www.ll.georgetown.edu/intl/guides/cyberspace/index.html
The law library at Georgetown University offers a research guide on cyberlaw prepared by the Department of Foreign and International Law.

http://www.temple.edu/lawschool/dpost/writings.html
Professor David Post has written extensively on cyberlaw.

http://www.cli.org
The Cyberspace Law Institute.

http://www.asil.org
The website of the American Society for International Law

http://www.usdoj.gov/criminal/cybercrime/intl.html
This U.S. website has extensive links dealing with international activities and legislation on cybercrime.

http://www.cdt.org/legislation/107th/wiretaps/
The website of the Centre for Democracy and Technology has pages dealing with legislation affecting the Internet.

http://www.gahtan.com/cyberlaw/
The website of a Canadian lawyer that posts "The Cyberlaw Encyclopedia".

INTERNATIONAL ORGANISATIONS

http://www.oecd.org//dsti/sti/it/secur
Documents and events relating to information security and privacy issues.

http://www.iccwbo.org
The Alliance against commercial cybercrime of the International Chamber of Commerce.

http://www.uncjin.org
The website of the United Nations Crime and Justice Information Network. It addresses
cyberspace issues.

http://www.odccp.org
The website of the United Nations Office for Drug Control and Crime Prevention

http://www.coe.int/
The Council of Europe Cybercrime Convention, issued in 2001 and adopted as a model by other countries. The text of the Convention can be found under Legal Affairs, fight against organized crime. There is no direct bookmark for downloading the document.

MISCELLANEOUS

http://cnet.com/enterprise/0-9567.html?tag=dir
A very informative web site with information technology and commerce related information. This is their security site.

http://www.infosecuritymag.com/
Information Security magazine is a recognised publication with news, analysis, insight and commentary on information security. The web site also offers an information security e-mail newsletter and an information security news web site.

http://www.linuxsecurity.com/
A great web site for offering information about security and the open source Linux operating system.

http://www.zdnet.com/enterprise/filters/resources/0,10227,600 7271,00.html

A very informative web site for people who want to buy, use, or learn more about technology. This is their security site.

http://www.epic.org
The Electronic Privacy Information Centre, includes a survey of national policies with regards to the use of encryption.

http://www.privacyinternational.org/
As above, a website discussing personal privacy issues

SECURITY MAILING LISTS

The following web pages are the "home" for some of the security mailing lists available. From these web pages you can subscribe to these mailing lists, search through mailing list archives, or find out about the mailing list itself.

BugTraq
http://www.securityfocus.com/
Home of the widely subscribed BugTraq mailing list, for announcements and detailed discussions of computer security vulnerabilities. And there are several other useful security-related mailing lists as well. The web site also has information on security basics, intrusion detection, incident response, and for Microsoft, Sun and Linux systems, as well as databases on vulnerabilities and viruses.

CERT Advisory
http://www.cert.org/contact_cert/certmaillist.html
A well-respected mailing list providing descriptions of serious security problems and their impact, along with instructions on how to obtain patches or details of work-arounds. In addition, the website has excellent resources for improving security practices and implementations. Highly recommended.

Crypto-Gram Newsletter
http://www.counterpane.com/crypto-gram.html
An excellent monthly newsletter on computer security and cryptography.

Executive Security Digest
http://www.securityportal.com/topnews/
A weekly executive-level summary of important information security news. Other interesting security mailing lists are also available.

Firewalls
http://www.lists.gnac.net/firewalls/
A mailing list for the discussion of Internet firewall security systems and related issues, including the design, construction, operation, maintenance, and philosophy of Internet firewall security systems. However, this is a very active mailing list and you will be inundated with postings.

NTBugtraq
http://www.ntbugtraq.com/
NTBugtraq is a mailing list for the discussion of security exploits and security bugs in Microsoft Windows NT and its related applications.

Security Alert Consensus
http://www.sans.org/sansnews

SANS Newsbites
http://www.sans.org/sansnews
SANS (System Administration, Networking and Security) Institute provides the "Security Alert Consensus", which is a weekly summary of new security alerts and recommended countermeasures, and the "SANS Newsbites", which is a weekly summary of information security news. The web site also has some excellent information security resources.

SECURITY PORTALS

http://www.infowar.com/
http://www.cerias.purdue.edu/coast/hotlist/
http://www.infosyssec.org/
http://www.itsecurity.com/
http://packetstorm.securify.com/

http://secinf.net/
http://www.securityfocus.com/
http://www.securityportal.com/
http://www.securitysearch.net/

SECURITY STANDARDS

http://www.diffuse.org/secure.html#help
The Diffuse project provides reference and guidance information on available and emerging standards and specifications that facilitate the electronic exchange of information, including a comprehensive listing of information security standards. A good starting point.

http://www.iso.ch/cate/d33441.html
ISO/IEC 17799:2000 Information technology -- Code of practice for information security management. This is an essential document, and its general content is dealt with extensively in this book.

http://www.bsi-global.com/group.xhtml
BS 7799-2:1999 Information security management --
Specification for information security management systems. Has very useful information.

http://www.standards.com.au/
AS/NZS 4444-2:1999 Information security management --
Specification for information security management systems.

http://www.itu.int
The International Telecommunications Union (ITU) produces recommendations that are developed and published as standards by the International Standards Organization (ISO) and the International Electrotechnical Commission (IEC). These include the X.509 standard for digital certificates and the X.800 series of standards for electronic commerce related activities.

http://www.ietf.org

The Internet Engineering Task Force is the major international forum for the discussion and development of Internet-related technical standards – the pages "IETF Security Area" were under construction in mid 2002.

http://csrc.nist.gov/publications/
The Computer Security Resource Center is maintained by the US Government National Institute of Standards and Technology. Good resource for US Government standards and other resources. This website also has links to the security standards activities of the Institution of Electrical and Electronic Engineers (IEEE), the European Computer Manufacturers Association (ECMA), also working on the development of security related standards as well as to the work of other bodies.

http://www.radium.ncsc.mil/tpep/
US Government Commercial Product Evaluations, with links to the "Common Criteria" (Common Criteria Information Technology Security Evaluation CCITSE), the "Rainbow Series" (Trusted Computer System Evaluation Criteria TCSEC) and the Evaluated Products List.

http://www.caspr.org
Work in progress to create a Common Body of Knowledge (CBK) through a series of Commonly Accepted Security Practices and Recommendations (CASPR). It is expected that this material will become available in late 2002.

http://www.sans.org
The System Administration and Networking Security Institute provides guidance, training and information on a broad range of information security matters.

http://www.issa.org
The Information Systems Security Association – a website primarily for information security professionals

http://www.gocsi.com/
The Computer Security Institute

http://www.itil-itsm-world.com/security.htm
The Information Technology Infrastructure Library (ITIL) originated in the UK Government's Central Computing and Communications Agency and developed since into an autonomous business unit providing documentation, guidance, consultancy and other activites

http://www.survive.com/
Worldwide professional association for business continuity professionals.

REFERENCE SITES

http://www.cs.georgetown.edu/~denning/publications.html
Professor Dorothy Denning's website, at Georgetown University, contains many documents and publications on cyber-crime, encryption and related matters, and constitutes a very good starting point.

http://whatis.techtarget.com/
An excellent on-line encyclopædia specifically for IT-related definitions. It has a topic specific index for security, among other topics.

http://www.cis.ohio-state.edu/hypertext/information/rfc.html
An index, and key word search, of Internet Request For Comments (RFC) documents, which are the written definitions of the protocols and policies of the Internet.

Some interesting, general RFCs on Internet security are:

RFC 1281: Guidelines for the Secure Operation of the Internet / R. D. Pethia, S. Crocker and B. Y. Fraser. - November 1991
http://www.cis.ohio-state.edu/htbin/rfc/rfc1281.html

RFC2084: Considerations for Web Transaction Security / G. Bossert, S. Cooper, W. Drummond - January 1997
http://www.cis.ohio-state.edu/htbin/rfc/rfc2084.html

RFC 2196: Site Security Handbook / B. Fraser, Editor - September 1997.
http://www.cis.ohio-state.edu/htbin/rfc/INDEX.rfc.html

RFC 2350: Expectations for Computer Security Incident Response / N. Brownlee, E. Guttman - June 1998.
http://www.cis.ohio-state.edu/htbin/rfc/rfc2350.html

RFC 2504: Users' Security Handbook. . Guttman, L. Leong, G. Malkin. February 1999.
http://www.cis.ohio-state.edu/htbin/rfc/rfc2504.html

RFC 2828: Internet Security Glossary. R. Shirey. May 2000
http://www.cis.ohio-state.edu/htbin/rfc/rfc2828.html

VENDORS

http://www.microsoft.com/security/
Microsoft Corporation's IT security website.

http://www.cisco.com/warp/public/779/largeent/issues/security/
Cisco Systems is the world-wide leading maker of data networking equipment for the Internet. This is their enterprise security website.

http://www.ibm.com/services/e-business/security.html
IBM develops and manufactures computers, networking systems, software, and other IT devices. They are the third largest company in terms of revenue and performance in the IT industry. This is their security and privacy website.

http://www.oracle.com/ip/solve/security/index.html
Oracle Corporation is a provider of software and services, primarily Internet enabled database, tools and application products. They are the fourth-largest company in terms of revenue and performance in the IT industry. This is their database security website.

http://www.sun.com/products-n-solutions/software/security/index.html
Sun Microsystems is a provider of Unix networked systems and are the fifth largest company (in terms of revenue and performance) in the IT industry. This is their computer security website.

http://www.checkpoint.com/
Check Point is a commercial provider of Firewall software and security solutions. They are the largest company in terms of revenue and performance in the security and encryption section of the IT industry.

http://www.verisign.com/
Verisign Incorporated is a commercial provider of Internet trust services including authentication, validation and payment needed to conduct secure electronic commerce and communications over the Internet. They are the second largest company in terms of revenue and performance in the security and encryption section of the IT industry.

http://www.symantec.com/
Symantec Corporation is a commercial provider of a broad range of content and network security solutions, including anti-viral software. They are the third largest company in terms of revenue and performance in the security and encryption section of the IT industry.

http://www.pgp.com
Suppliers of Pretty Good Privacy software that can be downloaded free for non-commercial use.

http://iss.net/
ISS Group is a commercial provider of security software and management solutions. They are the fourth-largest company in terms of revenue and performance in the security and encryption section of the IT industry. They have an excellent database ("X-Force") and other resources for computer threats and vulnerabilities.

VIRUS HOAXES

http://hoaxbusters.ciac.org/
US Department of Energy (US DOE) and Computer Incident Advisory Capability (CIAC) on Internet Hoaxes and chain letters.

http://vmyths.com/
A useful "independent" site on virus myths, misconceptions, and hoaxes by a self-proclaimed expert.

VIRUS INFORMATION

Computer Associates:
http://ca.com/virusinfo/encyclopedia/

F-Secure:
http://www.europe.datafellows.com/v-descs/

Network Associates:
http://vil.nai.com/vil/default.asp

Sophos:
http://www.sophos.com/virusinfo/analyses/

Symantec:
http://www.symantec.com/avcenter/vinfodb.html

Trend Micro
http://www.antivirus.com/vinfo/virusencyclo/

APPENDIX 2

GLOSSARY

Alias	A name that an entity uses in place of its real name, usually for the purpose of either anonymity or deception.
Anonymous login	An access control weakness in many Internet hosts that enables users to gain access to general-purpose or public services and resources (e.g. by allowing any user to transfer data using File Transfer Protocol) without having a pre-established, user-specific account (i.e., user name and secret password).
Asymmetric cryptography	A modern branch of cryptography (popularly known as "public-key cryptography") in which the algorithms employ a pair of keys (a public key and a private key) and use a different component of the pair for different steps of the algorithm.
Attack	An assault on system security from an intelligent threat, i.e., a deliberate attempt to evade security services and violate the security policy of a system. An "active attack" attempts to alter system resources or affect their operation. A "passive attack" attempts to learn or make use of information from the system but does not affect system resources. (see also: wiretapping.) An "inside attack" is initiated by an entity inside the security perimeter, i.e., an

| | entity authorized to access system resources who uses them in an unapproved way.

An "outside attack" is from outside the perimeter, by an unauthorized or illegitimate user of the system. On the Internet, potential outside attackers range from amateur pranksters to organized criminals, international terrorists, and hostile governments. |
|---|---|
| Authentic signature | A signature (particularly a digital signature) that can be trusted because it can be verified. (See: validate vs. verify.) |
| Back door | A hardware or software mechanism that
• provides access to a system and its resources by other than the usual procedure,
• was deliberately left in place by the system's designers or maintainers, and
• usually is not publicly known. (See: trap door.)

A back door need not have malicious intent; e.g., operating systems sometimes are shipped by the manufacturer with privileged accounts intended for use by field service technicians or the vendor's maintenance programmers. |
| Brute force | A method of attack that tries all possibilities, one-by-one. |
| Contingency plan | A plan for emergency response, backup operations, and post-disaster recovery as part of a security program which ensures availability of critical system resources |

	and facilitate continuity of operations in a crisis.
Cookie	An HTTP server, when sending data to a client, may send along a cookie, which the client retains after the HTTP connection closes.

A server can use this mechanism to maintain persistent client-side state information for HTTP-based applications, retrieving the state information in later connections. A cookie may include a description of the range of URLs for which the state is valid. Future requests made by the client in that range will also send the current value of the cookie to the server.

Cookies can be used to generate profiles of web usage habits, and thus may infringe on personal privacy. |
Cracker	Someone who tries to break the security of, and gain access to, someone else's system without being invited. (See also hacker)
Cryptography	The mathematical science that deals with transforming data to render its meaning unintelligible (i.e., to hide its semantic content), prevent its undetected alteration, or prevent its unauthorized use. If the transformation is reversible, cryptography also deals with restoring encrypted data to intelligible form.
Cut-and-paste attack	An active attack on the data integrity of cipher-text achieved by replacing sections of cipher-text with other cipher-text. The

	result appears to decrypt correctly but decrypts to plaintext forged to the satisfaction of the attacker.
Denial of service	The prevention of authorized access to a system resource or the delaying of system operations and functions.
Dictionary attack	A brute-force technique of trying all the words in some large, exhaustive list, for example, trying all possible passwords; or by encrypting some known plaintext phrase with all possible keys so that the key for any given encrypted message containing that phrase may be obtained by lookup.
Digital watermarking	Computing techniques for inseparably embedding unobtrusive marks or labels as bits in digital data--text, graphics, images, video, or audio--and for detecting or extracting the marks later.
Eavesdropping	Passive secret wiretapping i.e., without the knowledge of the originator or the intended recipients of the communication.
Entrapment	The deliberate planting of apparent flaws in a system for the purpose of detecting attempted penetrations or confusing an intruder about which flaws to exploit." (also called honey pot.)
Firewall	A gateway between networks that restricts data communication traffic to and from one of the connected networks (the one "behind" the firewall) to protect that network's resources against threats from the other networks ("outside" the

145

	firewall).
	A firewall is not always a single computer and may consist of filtering routers and proxy servers.
	The difficulty lies in defining criteria by which packets are denied passage through the firewall, because a firewall not only needs to keep intruders out, but also needs to let authorized users in and out.
Flooding	An attack that attempts to cause a failure in (especially, in the security of) a computer system or other data processing entity by providing more input than the entity can process properly. (See: denial of service.)
Hacker	Someone with an interest in computers, who enjoys experimenting with them. (See: cracker.)

The term originated in the 1960s and had the connotation of "someone who figures things out and makes something cool happen". Today, the term is frequently misused, especially by journalists. |
| Handle (noun) | An on-line pseudonym, particularly one used by a cracker; derived from citizens band radio culture. |
| Hijack attack | A form of active wiretapping in which the attacker seizes control of a previously established communication association. (See also: man-in-the-middle attack, page-jacking, piggyback attack.) |

Intelligent threat	A situation where an adversary has the technical and operational capability to detect and exploit a vulnerability and also has the demonstrated, presumed, or inferred intent to do so. (See: threat.)
Intruder	An entity that gains or attempts to gain access to a system or system resource without having authorization to do so. (See: cracker.)
Intrusion detection	A security service that monitors and analyzes system events for the purpose of finding, and providing real-time or near real- time warning of, attempts to access system resources in an unauthorized manner.
Logic bomb	Malicious logic that activates when specified conditions are met. Usually intended to cause denial of service or otherwise damage system resources. (See: Trojan horse, virus, worm.)
Malicious logic	Hardware, software, or firmware intentionally included or inserted in a system for a harmful purpose. (See: logic bomb, Trojan horse, virus, worm.)
Malware	A contraction of "malicious software". (See: malicious logic.)
Man-in-the-middle	An active wiretapping attack in which the attacker intercepts and selectively modifies communicated data in order to masquerade as one or more of the entities involved in a communication association. (See: hijack attack, piggyback attack.)

Masquerade attack	An attack in which one system illegitimately assumes the identity of another entity. (See: spoofing attack.)
Page-jacking	Contraction of "Web page hijacking". A masquerade attack in which the attacker copies (steals) a home page or other material from the target server, re-hosts the page on a server the attacker controls, and causes the re-hosted page to be indexed by the major Web search services, thereby diverting browsers from the target server to the attacker's server.
Password sniffing	Passive wiretapping, usually on a local area network, to gain knowledge of passwords. (See: (usage note under) sniffing.)
Penetration	Successful, repeatable, unauthorized access to a protected system resource. (See: attack, violation.)
Penetration test	A system test, often part of system certification, in which evaluators attempt to circumvent the security features of the system.
Phreaking	Contraction of "phone break in". An attack on or penetration of a telephone system or any other communication or information system.
Piggyback attack	A form of active wiretapping where the attacker gains access to a system via intervals of inactivity in another user's legitimate communication connection. Sometimes called a "between- the-lines" attack. (See also: hijack attack, man-in-the-middle attack.)

Ping of death	An attack that sends an improperly large echo request packet (a "ping") with the intent of overflowing the input buffers of the destination machine and causing it to crash.
Ping sweep	An attack that sends echo requests ("pings") to a range of IP addresses, with the goal of finding hosts that can be probed for vulnerabilities.
Pretty Good Privacy/PGP ™	Trademarks of Network Associates, Inc., referring to a computer program (and related protocols) that uses cryptography to provide data security for electronic mail and other applications on the Internet.
Proxy server	A computer process often used as part of a firewall that relays a protocol between client and server computer systems, by appearing to the client to be the server and appearing to the server to be the client. In a firewall, a proxy server usually runs on a host, which may support proxies for several protocols (e.g., FTP, HTTP, and TELNET). Instead of a protected client connecting directly to an external server, the internal client connects to the proxy server that in turn connects to the external server. The proxy server waits for a request from inside the firewall, forwards the request to the remote server outside the firewall, gets the response, and then sends the response back to the client.

Reflection attack	A type of replay attack in which transmitted data is sent back to its originator.
Replay attack	An attack in which a valid data transmission is maliciously or fraudulently repeated, either by the originator or by an adversary who intercepts the data and retransmits it, possibly as part of a masquerade attack. (See: active wiretapping.)
Repudiation	Denial by a party involved in an electronic transaction of having participated in the transaction.
Secure Sockets Layer (SSL)	An Internet protocol (originally developed by Netscape Communications, Inc.) that uses connection-oriented end-to-end encryption to provide data confidentiality service and data integrity service for traffic between a client (often a web browser) and a server. Secure Sockets Layer can optionally provide peer entity authentication between the client and the server.
Security intrusion	A security event, or a combination of multiple security events, that constitutes a security incident in which an intruder gains, or attempts to gain, access to a system (or system resource) without having authorization to do so.
Smurf	Software that mounts a denial-of-service attack ("smurfing") by exploiting IP broadcast addressing and ICMP ping packets to cause flooding.

Social engineering	A euphemism for non-technical or low-technology means--such as lies, impersonation, tricks, bribes, blackmail, and threats, used to attack information systems. (See: masquerade attack.)
Spam	(1.) Verb: To indiscriminately send unsolicited, unwanted, irrelevant, or inappropriate messages, especially commercial advertising in mass quantities. (2.) Noun: electronic "junk mail".
Spoofing attack	A synonym for "masquerade attack".
Star Trek attack	An attack that penetrates your system where no attack has ever gone before.
Steganography	Methods of hiding the existence of a message or other data. This is different than cryptography, which hides the meaning of a message but does not hide the message itself.
Tamper	Make an unauthorized modification in a system to alter or degrade the security services that the system was intended to provide.
Threat	A potential for violation of security, which exists when there is a circumstance, capability, action, or event that could breach security and cause harm.
Trap door	A hidden computer flaw known to an intruder, or a hidden computer mechanism (usually software) installed by an intruder, who can activate the trap door to gain access to the computer

	without being blocked by security services or mechanisms. (See also: back door, Trojan horse.)
Trojan horse	A computer program that appears to have a useful function, but also has a hidden and potentially malicious function that evades security mechanisms, sometimes by exploiting legitimate authorizations of a system entity that invokes the program.
Virus	A hidden, self-replicating section of computer software, usually malicious logic, that propagates by infecting--i.e., inserting a copy of itself into and becoming part of—another program. A virus cannot run by itself; it requires that its host program be run in order to become active.
Vulnerability	A flaw or weakness in a system's design, implementation, or operation and management that could be exploited to violate the system's security policy. Most systems have vulnerabilities of some sort, but this does not mean that the systems are too flawed to use. Not every threat results in an attack, and not every attack succeeds. Success depends on the degree of vulnerability, the strength of attacks, and the effectiveness of any countermeasures in use.
War dialer	A computer program that automatically dials a series of telephone numbers to find lines connected to computer systems, and catalogues those numbers so that a cracker can try to break into the systems.

Wiretapping	An attack that intercepts and accesses data and other information contained in a flow in a communication system. Originally, the term applied to a mechanical connection to an electrical conductor. It now refers to reading information from any medium used for a link or even directly from a node, gateway or switch.
Worm	A computer program that can run independently, can propagate a complete working version of itself onto other hosts on a network, and may consume computer resources destructively.